60p

Scottish Independence

Weighing Up the Economics

Gavin McCrone has studied, written and lectured about the Scottish economy over a period of many years. He was a Fellow and Tutor in economics at Brasenose College, Oxford, in the 1960s. He then spent two decades as Chief Economic Adviser to successive Secretaries of State for Scotland. He was successively head of two Scottish Government Departments – the Industry Department for Scotland and the Scottish Development Department. He returned to his previous career in the 1990s as a professor of economics, first at Glasgow University and then at the Edinburgh University Business School. He is a Fellow of the Royal Society of Edinburgh and was a Vice President of the Society from 2002 to 2005.

Scottish Independence

Weighing Up the Economics

Gavin McCrone

BIRLINN

First published in 2013 by
Birlinn Limited
West Newington House
10 Newington Road
Edinburgh
EH9 1QS

www.birlinn.co.uk

ISBN: 978 1 78027 159 0

British Library Cataloguing-in-Publication Data
A catalogue record for this book is available from the British Library

Typeset by Iolaire Typesetting, Newtonmore
Printed and bound by Grafica Veneta
www.graficaveneta.com

To my family, for whom Scotland's future is important

Contents

Foreword

As the date for a referendum on Scottish independence grows closer, arguments for and against what would amount to the greatest constitutional change in Britain for more than 300 years have grown intense. A sense of something approaching national anxiety can be discerned as Scots of every persuasion seek answers to the fundamental questions that will govern the outcome before they go to the polls in September 2014. Would an independent Scotland be worse or better off? More pertinently, perhaps, would it have the capacity to flourish? Or would the ending of the Union expose the country to growing hardship at a time of economic uncertainty?

Professor Gavin McCrone brings more than 40 years' experience to bear on these crucial issues. As an academic and, for many years, a senior civil servant, he has been at the heart of economic planning in Scotland – most significantly as Chief Economic Adviser to the Scottish Office from 1970 to 1992 – for much of his career.

He approaches the subject from an objective standpoint, examining each aspect with a strong command of statistics and a dispassionate assessment of their merits. More importantly, perhaps, he comes unswayed by bias. On the one hand, he has advised successive United Kingdom governments on economic policy – a background synonymous with the constitutional status quo. On the other hand, as a senior civil servant in 1974, he compiled a report for ministers on whether North Sea oil revenues would allow an independent Scotland to manage financially. He concluded not only that they would but that they had the capacity to transform the country's fortunes. His paper remained confidential at the time but, if it had been publicly available, the course of Scottish politics might have been very different.

So neither side can afford to ignore Professor McCrone's analysis. He is, in journalistic terms, 'a reliable source'. More than that, he has the great merit of clarity. He examines each aspect of the independence debate with a combination of straightforward analysis and simply expressed conclusions, providing the bare minimum of statistics, set out in a helpfully comprehensible style.

He addresses head on the questions that most trouble voters – whether floating or not. How wealthy a nation is Scotland? How dependent would it be on oil revenues? Would independence allow the country sufficient flexibility on taxation to bolster its economy? Could it afford to fund the welfare state on which it has grown to depend? Would it gain rapid entry to the EU and, if so, would it have to join the euro? What are the implications of adopting the pound as its currency? Could an independent Scotland have weathered the collapse of its once powerful banks? How viable is its energy policy? Above all, is North Sea oil the key that would unlock its potential or is it a diminishing and unreliable asset?

In addition to these critical issues, Professor McCrone examines the case for other options facing the nation: differing forms of devolution such as the proposals contained in the current Scotland Act; the so-called Devo-Max plan for full-scale fiscal independence; and its less extreme version, Devo-Plus. He questions the assumptions behind each, making the important point that they would all, in different ways, impinge on other areas of the United Kingdom – not always to beneficial effect – and goes on to develop his own favoured alternative.

The backcloth to these arguments is a decision which will

confront every person of voting age living in Scotland. It is a more fundamental one than any they have voted on before. Unlike a general election, where the choice, however far-reaching, can be changed in five years' time, this one is irreversible. If Scotland does, indeed, secede from the United Kingdom to form an independent state, it cannot then decide to rejoin if the outcome is not to its liking. Equally, if the decision is to remain part of the United Kingdom, then that too is one that will endure for many years – 'at least for a generation', in the words of the First Minister, Alex Salmond; and, if any attempt were made to revisit it more frequently than that, it would, in all likelihood, be strongly resisted by the other countries of the UK because it would be destabilising for all of them.

It is therefore important that the implications of this critical choice are fully understood by those who will make it. While many people will rest their decision on personal or emotional grounds, opting perhaps to stay within the United Kingdom because of family connections or historical legacy, others will feel equally strongly that it is precisely this history that urges them towards the re-establishment of an independent Scottish nation.

Whatever the reasons influencing their vote, it is important that everyone who takes part in the referendum has a clear understanding of the implications for Scotland and the rest of the United Kingdom. They need answers to the questions that have arisen on the way towards the final decision and clear guidance on how best these can be answered. This book provides the road map that should be the essential companion for all those charged with deciding the future direction of their country.

Magnus Linklater
June 2013

Preface

In 1707 when the members of the Scottish and English Parliaments passed the Act of Union, parliaments were very far from being representative of the people. But, in 2014, it will be for every person of voting age living in Scotland to decide on their country's constitutional future.

There are many Scots living in other parts of the United Kingdom or abroad who have views on this matter and feel they should have been able to vote. But, apart from the major complications that would introduce, I agree with the view taken by the Scottish and UK governments that it is right for people living in Scotland to be the ones taking the decision. It is they who will live with the consequences of that decision, whatever it may be.

I have no doubt that Scotland could prosper either as an independent country or if it chooses to remain part of the United Kingdom. But the consequences will be substantial whichever way the decision goes. So long as the issues are properly understood – or at least as well understood as the available information allows – there should be no complaint with the decision. This book weighs up the economic issues – it does not attempt to deal with other important issues, such as defence. It is in the belief that many economic aspects of the decision are not well understood, because people lack the information that they need, that I have written this book.

I have never been a member of a political party and I

am beholden to no person or group. I have tried to be as objective as possible in setting out the issues. I realise that this will not satisfy everyone. There will inevitably be those who will disagree with some of the judgements I make. But, if so, I hope that the arguments can be assessed on their merits rather than on the basis of preconceived ideas. In the following pages, there will be criticism of arguments put forward by the present Scottish government, but there will also be plenty of criticism of what Westminster governments have said and done.

As I write, the independence debate is constantly developing. Scarcely a day goes by without either some change in government policy, a fresh set of statistics, the publication of a report on the subject or just comment in the press. Other books are being published or are planned. I should make it clear therefore that this book went to the publisher at the end of March 2013 and I have not been able to offer an opinion or comment on anything that was published after that date.

I am grateful to Jeremy Peat, Professor David Bell and Sir David Edward, who have each read chapters, and to my son, Angus, who has read much of the book. All have offered valuable comments. Any errors or omissions that remain, however, are my responsibility alone. I am also grateful to my wife who has uncomplainingly tolerated the many hours I have spent absenting myself from other activities to be in my study writing this book.

Gavin McCrone
June 2013

1

How Well Off Are We?

Economic arguments have formed a large part of the SNP's case for independence, ever since the growth in support for their party in the late 1960s. For an independence movement this is unusual, although it appears now also to be a factor in Catalonia. Most commonly, when countries split to form independent states, it is because of differences in culture or serious grievances about the way they have been treated. Whatever the economic consequences, they take the view that they simply do not want any longer to be part of the larger state with which they have been associated. There have been numerous examples – the breakup of the Soviet Union, the collapse of Yugoslavia and even the independence of what then became the Irish Free State and is now the Irish Republic. In this latter case, although the economic condition of Ireland within the UK during much of the previous century and right up to the First World War certainly gave grounds for serious grievance, even there, as with the other countries, little if any detailed argument about the economic consequences of independence or the policies that a separate state might pursue took place. Indeed, what really seems to have brought the issue to a head in Ireland was not so much its economy as the savage and ill-judged reaction of the UK government to the 1916 uprising in Dublin, which resulted in many of the leaders being executed.

Scotland has its own distinct culture and history. More-over, during my lifetime I have witnessed the development of a growing awareness of Scotland's separate identity and the confidence that goes with that. Nevertheless, it is not so difficult to understand why the argument about the economy features as much as it does in the Scottish context. Scotland had its industrial revolution early and, during those years, the economy grew rapidly. But this early success left a legacy of problems that was to dominate the economy for much of the 20th century, as it did also in the north of England and South Wales, when the traditional industries of coal, steel, textiles and shipbuilding, together with associated engineering, went into decline. While, in the post-war decades, unemployment remained low by present day or pre-war standards, it was frequently twice the rate for the UK and net emigration was extremely high, amounting over the decades of the 1950s and 1960s to a total of 609,000. Approximately half of this was to the rest of the UK and half overseas. This was equivalent to 30 per cent more than the whole population of Edinburgh.[1] There were serious problems of deprivation in some of the industrial areas, notably in the west of Scotland – a problem that persists to this day. Scotland was, of course, not the only part of the UK suffering these problems. But they gave rise to a feeling in Scotland that the country's economy was somehow not doing as well as it should and that the UK government in London was not doing enough.

The UK government, through its regional development policy, especially during the 1960s and 1970s, when this policy was at its height with substantial funds devoted to it, attempted to deal with this problem. In addition to substantial grants available to encourage industrial investment in areas of high unemployment, the Highlands and Islands Development Board (HIDB) was set up in 1965 and the Scottish Development Agency (SDA) in 1975. Considerable success was achieved through the introduction of new industries, most notably, but by no means exclusively, electronics. Indeed,

Scotland was the most successful part of the UK in attracting inward investment from overseas and, after Ireland, one of the most successful in Europe. But this did not eliminate the problem and the success with investment in the electronics industry received a severe setback after 2000, when the industry encountered a recession and much of the new investment went to countries with lower labour costs. What had been achieved was not always recognised and the details of successive regional development policies were largely lost on the general public. After the 1979 election, the new Conservative government's philosophy was against intervention and in favour of giving full rein to market forces. Assistance through regional policy was scaled down, though it still continues, as do SDA and HIDB. But both of these agencies were significantly modified in the early 1990s and renamed Scottish Enterprise and Highlands and Islands Enterprise. Their scope and remit were again changed by the SNP government after its election in 2007.

The election of 1979 was followed by a period of severe economic difficulty in Scotland, as it was also in many parts of England, especially in the north. The tight monetary policies followed by the government resulted in the closure of many industrial firms, not only those in the older heavy industries of shipbuilding, steel, coal and heavy engineering but also some inward investment companies, the motor industry at Bathgate and Linwood, the aluminium smelter at Invergordon and many new businesses that had set up in Scotland. It was at this time that Scotland lost much of its manufacturing industry.

It was ironic that, as North Sea oil production began to flow in substantial quantities, it also adversely affected much of Scotland's existing manufacturing through strengthening the UK's balance of payments and pushing up the exchange rate for the pound, so that many businesses became uncompetitive.

Indeed, in these years, the decline of existing industry appeared to outweigh the very welcome benefits to companies that took advantage of the opportunities available from oil-related activity. I thought at the time that policies were needed to try to counter this adverse effect because, even if much of this was inevitable, it resulted in high unemployment and great distress. The result was that the unemployment rate in Scotland peaked at just under 14 per cent in 1986 – much higher even than in the recent severe recession.[2]

The sense of grievance stemming from the difficulties in the economy in past decades has therefore been a major factor in the growth of support for independence, even if now Scotland's performance relative to the rest of the United Kingdom is significantly improved. Some people felt that Scotland's economic performance, as part of the UK, was below its potential and started to question whether it might do better on its own.

This feeling received a major boost when North Sea oil and gas were discovered in the 1970s. The vast bulk of the oil discoveries (though not the gas) were off the Scottish coast and, under international rules, would have been in Scotland's offshore territory were it an independent state. The importance of this seemed at first to be underestimated by the UK government and it was some time before appropriate policies to give benefit to the state were put in place but, once this was done, the revenues from taxation were very large indeed and of major benefit to the UK Exchequer. No longer did it seem so persuasive to the general public to argue that Scots would be worse off if their country became independent. It was no surprise therefore that support for independence grew.

How Wealthy is Scotland?

Scotland's relative economic position within the UK is now enormously better than it was in the early 1970s. The strength of an economy is assessed by using statistics that measure the total of goods and services produced. Two measures are widely used – gross domestic product (GDP) and gross value added (GVA). The difference between the two is not important so long comparisons are consistent.* Scotland's gross value added (GVA) per head, at 98.6 per cent of the UK average in 2011, was exceeded only by London and the South East of England (Table 1). At a lower level of aggregation, the north east of Scotland is now one of the most prosperous parts of the UK with a GVA per head of 144 per cent of the UK average, second only to Inner London. This compares with the situation in the late 1950s and 1960s when Scotland's GDP per head was around 10 per cent below the UK average and in some years even lower, making it one of the poorest parts of the UK.[3] In contrast, Wales and the Northern Region of England both seem to have fallen somewhat further behind over the same period, with GVA per head 75.2 per cent and 75.9 per cent of the UK average respectively. Net migration is now into, rather than out of, Scotland and unemployment at the latest count was fractionally below the UK average.[4] This turnaround is partly a consequence of the 1960s and 1970s regional policies, including the work of Scottish Enterprise and Highlands and Islands Enterprise, but also the remarkable growth in Scotland of the financial services sector and employment across a range of industries associated with the development of North Sea oil and gas, especially in the

* GDP relates to output, including sales taxes but not any subsidies, whereas GVA is output excluding indirect taxes but including any subsidies. As indirect taxes are more important than subsidies, GDP figures for Scotland are somewhat higher than GVA. Official statistics now most frequently use GVA whereas, in earlier years, only GDP was available. The reader may find this confusing – some of the comparisons are made in GDP and some in GVA but that is how they are published by the government statisticians.

North East. In addition the decline of the older industries has now reduced them to a size where they are no longer such a drag on the performance of the economy.

Scotland is therefore quite a wealthy country, whether compared with the rest of the United Kingdom or internationally, because the United Kingdom itself is one of the wealthier countries in Europe and indeed the world. Alex Salmond has claimed that, if Scotland was independent, it would be the sixth wealthiest country per head, based on OECD statistics.[5] He arrives at this conclusion by adding to Scotland's GDP a Scottish geographical share of the output of the North Sea. This increases Scottish GDP by some 21 per cent[6] and results in Scotland's GDP per head being exceeded in Europe only by Luxembourg, Norway, Switzerland and Monaco.

However this should not be accepted without qualification. In the first place, he uses Scotland's share of the North Sea as estimated by Professor Alex Kemp of Aberdeen University, which would give Scotland about 90 per cent of the output and tax revenue.[7] The whole of the UK's offshore area has hitherto been treated for statistical purposes as a separate area and without any divisions. Kemp's estimate is derived by applying the international rules for division of offshore territory between states. It is the best estimate one can get but, as he himself points out, it is not something that is agreed by the rest of the United Kingdom. Negotiations would therefore be needed, as they frequently are between countries, and that may not prove such a simple matter.

Secondly, GDP from oil and gas includes the profits of the oil companies and the income of those working offshore. Company profits will be distributed to shareholders, the majority of whom are not resident in Scotland, and some of those working offshore also come from other parts of the UK. All of that would be taken account of were we to have estimates of Gross *National* Product (GNP), where income paid abroad and income received from abroad are both calculated to give a net figure, but no allowance for this is made in GDP. Unfortunately GNP is much more difficult to estimate and no such estimates have been made for Scotland. The truth of the matter is that Scotland's GDP would, indeed, be some 21 per cent higher, if the output of the North Sea were included but, leaving aside tax revenue, which is dealt with in the next part of this chapter, it would not make much difference to the living standards of people in Scotland.

Table 1
Gross Value Added in 2011 by Country and Region

	GVA per head Index UK = 100	Growth in total GVA since 2010 %	Share of UK total GVA %
United Kingdom	100.0	2.4	100.0
England	102.3	2.3	83.9
North East	75.9	1.5	3.1
North West	85.1	1.9	9.2
Yorkshire and Humber	81.6	1.9	6.8
East Midlands	86.6	2.1	6.1
West Midlands	83.8	2.0	7.1
East of England	92.7	2.9	8.5
London	170.7	2.1	21.1
South East	107.2	3.1	14.3
South West	91.5	2.3	7.6
Scotland	98.6	1.9	8.1
Wales	75.2	2.2	3.5
Northern Ireland	79.2	2.5	2.2

Source: Office of National Statistics, December 2012

Nevertheless, the argument for independence on economic grounds is still made. Scotland's growth is compared unfavourably with other countries of similar size, many of which have quite different economic circumstances. It is also compared unfavourably with the UK, where growth of output (as measured by GDP or GVA) has been faster than in Scotland over a long period; but this ignores the fact that it is not the growth of output in aggregate but output per head that is a guide to the wellbeing of the population. Inward migration has been much higher in the south of England than in Scotland and it is therefore not surprising that output in aggregate has risen faster for the UK as a whole than for Scotland. But, at the same time, the gap in output per head has narrowed so that in Scotland it is now almost equal to the UK average, showing that Scotland's position has improved when compared with the UK as a whole.

Does Scotland Pay its Way?

Taxes across the United Kingdom, apart from those that are the responsibility of local authorities, are collected by HM Revenue and Customs on behalf of the Treasury. Apart from local authority taxation, tax rates are the same across all countries and regions of the UK, although this may change when, under the recent Scotland Act, the Scottish government becomes responsible for part of income tax. The amount of revenue raised in the various parts of the UK therefore depends mainly on their respective wealth and level of incomes. Public expenditure, on the other hand, is disbursed without any regard for wealth, incomes or tax revenue of a particular part of the UK, with the aim of giving a broadly comparable level of public service. This ought to be related in some way to need and, in the case of spending programmes such as social protection that are UK wide, this will be the case.

Under this system, there is no need to take account of how far revenue raised in any part of the UK covers the public expenditure in that country or region, since the budget is framed for the UK as a whole. It is not easy, therefore, to establish for which regions or countries expenditure is higher than the revenue raised and for which it is lower. Although there have been a number of academic studies that have given estimates, until recently there were no official estimates except for Scotland. The Silk Commission on devolution in Wales and the Northern Ireland executive have, however, now produced figures for their territories and both show much larger fiscal deficits than for Scotland.[8] In Wales, public expenditure per head, though higher than the UK average, is not as high as for Scotland but, reflecting the lower GDP per head, tax revenue is much lower, and, for Northern Ireland, expenditure per head is higher than for Scotland, while revenue per head, as for Wales, is lower. No official estimates have been published for English regions, except for identifiable public expenditure. These show that the northern region of England also had public expenditure per head above the UK average and, since its GDP per head was similar to that of Wales, I would expect it also to have a substantial fiscal deficit.

The Scottish Office and, following devolution, the Scottish government have published annual estimates of government expenditure and revenue since 1991 with figures that go back to 1986. It is far from a straightforward task. While the Treasury publishes figures for 'identifiable expenditure' by country and region, this cannot include those items such as defence, foreign embassies and interest on the National Debt for which there is no breakdown. A share of these items can only be allocated using some ratio such as population. The revenue side is even more difficult. Many people living in Scotland and companies operating in Scotland are not taxed in Scotland but in some other part of the UK. The revenue which relates to Scotland is derived from information collected by HM Revenue and Customs but has to be estimated. The resulting figures have been criticised, especially by the SNP in the early years. However they have been much improved, are now the responsibility of the SNP government and give as clear a picture of Scotland's present budgetary position as can be obtained.

What they show is that taxation revenue from Scotland is approximately equal to its population share of the UK. This is not surprising given that Scotland's GDP per head is only very slightly below the UK average. But public expenditure per head is over 10 per cent above the average for the UK (see Table 2).[9] It has been above the UK average for many years, certainly going back to the 1960s and, according to my calculations, even earlier.[10] In the 1960s, there was a deliberate decision by the then Conservative government to increase public expenditure in Scotland and in the northeast of England, because of their difficult economic circumstances and need for development.[11] The extent to which Scotland's public expenditure per head has been above the UK average seems to have narrowed over the years, from about 20 per cent above in the 1990s to 15 per cent above in the mid 2000s and 10 per cent above in the latest year. But comparisons are difficult because improvements have been made in the methodology. In earlier years, the comparison was only based on 'identifiable' expenditure but, in recent years, the estimates have included a population share of defence, national debt interest and international services. This larger denominator narrows the gap and makes it difficult to get a continuous series of figures on a consistent basis. Using the Scottish government's figures for identifiable expenditure only, the gap will still appear to be of the order of 14 per cent.[12]

Before 1979, Scotland's share of public expenditure was determined as a result of annual discussions between the Secretary of State for Scotland and the Chief Secretary to the Treasury. But, since 1979, it has mainly been determined by the Barnett formula and comes in the form of a block grant. The workings of this formula are obscure to most people. But in fact the Barnett formula is quite simple. It is no more than the application of Scotland's population ratio to that of England to determine any change in public expenditure that Scotland receives when public expenditure increases or decreases in England. As such it was thought by many people, myself included, that it would result in a gradual narrowing of the gap between public expenditure per head in Scotland and the UK average. This has been referred to as the Barnett squeeze.

In the event, this has not happened as rapidly as expected. This is due to several factors. First, the formula is only applied to the annual change in public expenditure and this is quite small when compared with the inherited amount from previous years. The formula does not adjust the inherited amount at all, even if there were a decline in the Scottish population. Secondly, it relates only to the part of public spending controlled by the Scottish government and not even to all of that, since expenditure on agriculture is separately determined. The biggest single component of public expenditure in Scotland is social protection, which is the responsibility of the UK government and is not subject to the formula at all. This exceeds spending on health and education combined, the two largest programmes funded by the Scottish government. Thirdly, the formula has, on occasion, been bypassed if there seemed a pressing need to do so – for example, if there was a national negotiation on wages in some sector of public service such as the NHS.

The upshot is that Scottish public expenditure per head

was still £1,197 per head higher than the UK average in 2011–12.[13] This not only results in expenditure being substantially higher than tax revenue (excluding tax revenue from the North Sea) but is a source of periodic and growing complaint in England, where it is taken to mean that Scotland is subsidised by the UK. Only if public expenditure in the various parts of the UK was seen to be clearly related to need could it be properly defended against such complaints. But no needs assessment has been carried out since a Treasury study in the late 1970s. This was done then in preparation for the devolution scheme in the 1970s, which was never implemented. It appeared to show that, at the time, Scottish public expenditure was indeed higher than an assessment of need would justify. Scotland obviously does have special needs – particularly the higher costs associated with providing services in remote communities with a scattered population and the poor health record and deprivation in some urban areas, especially in the west of Scotland. But incomes in Scotland are now much closer to the UK average than in the 1970s, when the assessment was done, and, although in the absence of an up-to-date needs assessment no firm conclusion can be drawn, it seems unlikely that it would fully justify the level of public expenditure that Scotland currently receives as compared with other parts of the UK.

The counterpart of the Calman Commission in Scotland, which led to the enhanced powers for the Scottish government contained in the 2012 Scotland Act, was the Holtham Commission in Wales.[14] Using the formula used for distributing public expenditure in England and applying it to Wales and Scotland, Holtham concluded that Wales, although also receiving public expenditure per head above the UK average, received too small a share of UK public expenditure and Scotland too much. This was largely because Scotland's income per head (as measured by GDP) was much higher than that of Wales, which was well below the UK average.

If this were all there was to this subject, one would have to conclude that the government of an independent Scotland, responsible for all taxation and public expenditure, would find itself with a very substantial budget deficit, amounting to 14.6 per cent of GDP in 2011–12 according to the Scottish government's own figures in *Government Expenditure and Revenue Scotland 2011–12* (GERS). But that takes no account of revenue from North Sea oil which would accrue to an independent Scotland. If the revenue from the geographical share that would belong to Scotland as an independent state is included, following Kemp's analysis, this reduces the deficit to 8.1 per cent of GDP in 2010–11 and to 5.0 per cent in 2011–12 – still high but less than the UK deficit of 7.9 per cent in the same year.

Table 2

Total Public Expenditure Per Capita – Scotland and UK 2007–08 to 2011–12

	2007–08	2008–09	2009–10	2010–11	2011–12
Scotland (£)	10,786	11,302	11,829	12,133	12,134
UK (£)	9,497	10,184	10,764	11,008	10,937
Difference	1,289	1,118	1,065	1,125	1,197
Relative UK=100	*113.6*	*110.0*	*109.9*	*110.2*	*110.9*

Source: Government Expenditure and Revenue Scotland 2011–12, *March 2013*

Both of these deficits are, of course, unsustainable. They are a consequence of the financial crash of 2008 and the recession that followed. This caused tax revenue to fall and expenditure on benefits to rise as unemployment increased.

The austerity measures imposed by the UK government are intended to get the UK deficit down but the economy has shrunk, partly as a consequence of the austerity, and economic growth has been badly affected, so that the targets for reducing the deficit have become elusive.

But how realistic is the Scottish figure for the deficit of 5.0 per cent? It is of course hypothetical since, as part of the UK, Scotland does not have to balance its public revenue and expenditure. Alex Salmond has said that it shows that Scotland is in a stronger financial position than the UK. Is that really so? A number of qualifications have to be made.

In the first place, it is still a deficit and a deficit that is unsustainable. If Scotland had to balance its own budget, measures would be required to reduce it. Secondly, it is dependent on a geographical share of North Sea revenues accruing to Scotland. A more detailed discussion of the importance of North Sea oil will be found in Chapter 7. Suffice it to say here that there are many uncertainties. The Scottish government's assumptions about the North Sea, as explained earlier, use the geographical share of the North Sea based on the median line as estimated by Professor Alex Kemp but, as he himself said in evidence to the House of Commons Committee on Energy and Climate Change, the median line would be taken as the starting point and negotiations would follow, as they have done with other countries bordering the British part of the sea.[15] All this would take time and could involve arbitration.

Whatever the outcome of such negotiations, the revenues from the North Sea are of course substantial but they are also very volatile, depending on the output from the North Sea in any one year, on the price of oil and on the profits made by the oil companies. They have varied from about £1 billion a year to over £12 billion. At their peak in the early 1980s, they were very large indeed whereas, from the mid 1980s, when the price fell sharply, they were much reduced and, in the early 1990s, would have been insufficient, had they accrued to Scotland, to cover the fiscal deficit. Even over the last three years, they have shown great volatility from £12.9 billion in 2008–09, falling to £6.5 billion in 2009–10 and rising again to £8.8 billion in 2010–11 and £11.3 billion in 2011–12. For the future, one can only speculate. Oil production peaked in 1999 and, although it is expected to remain substantial for many years, it is now well below its peak level and expected gradually to decline. Revenue depends of course not just on output but also on the price and prices have proved very volatile. For the future, the outlook for prices is particularly uncertain – on the one hand, the rapid development of countries such as China and India may push prices up but, on the other, the exploitation of shale gas, which is now a major factor in the United States and may become one in Europe, could keep them down. Even if, as many expect, prices stay high, profitability may fall as companies exploit more marginal fields and the costs mount of removing structures from fields that have ceased production. These various factors are discussed in Chapter 7 but they have led the Office for Budget Responsibility to forecast quite a steep fall in tax revenues for the years ahead.

It is the stated policy of the present Scottish government that, when conditions allow, the North Sea revenues, or at least a proportion of them, would be paid into a special fund.[16] In this, they are influenced by the example of Norway, which set up such a fund in 1990. This too is discussed in Chapter 7. Given the likely variability in revenue from taxation on oil, putting the proceeds into a special fund would mean that its volatility would not affect the annual budget. It also makes sense because using oil revenues to finance ordinary public expenditure amounts to running down a capital asset to finance current spending.

But, while paying the North Sea revenues into such a fund would be very desirable, the government of an independent Scotland could not do without this revenue to finance its budget, so long as the balance between expenditure and revenue remained as it is now. Setting North Sea revenue aside for a special fund would therefore only mean that even more draconian steps would have to be taken to eliminate the budget deficit. In the longer run, the situation may be different – one would hope so – but this would require quite a transformation in the Scottish economy, either by reducing the need for such a high level of public expenditure or somehow increasing other tax receipts through economic growth.

There is a further uncertainty over the balance in what would become the budget of an independent Scotland. The figures in *Government Expenditure and Revenue Scotland 2011–2012* allocate the UK's interest payments on the National Debt on a per capita basis. For an independent Scotland, the National Debt would first have to be split with the rest of the UK. It could be done on a per capita basis but this might be resisted by the UK government on the grounds that, as Scotland's GDP was increased by the addition of output from the North Sea, it would be reasonable to allocate the National Debt by the share of GDP. That would make it some 21 per cent higher than a per capita allocation.

The GERS estimate for interest on the National Debt in 2011–12 was £4,072 million but, if it was split by GDP, including the North Sea share, it would raise the interest cost to around £4,930 million. There would also be uncertainty over the rate of interest that a Scottish government would have to pay. It probably would not be, as assumed in GERS, the same rate of interest as for the UK. Theoretically, the rate of interest on Scottish debt might be either higher or

lower than for the rest of the UK. But the rate on UK debt
is currently at a historic low and there must be doubt over
whether this would be matched for Scottish debt, unless
agreement was reached to issue common sterling bonds for
both countries. That would require stringent conditions on
fiscal policy to be met that satisfied both countries. Otherwise, as a newly independent country, Scotland would have
to establish its credibility as a borrower, not only with the
rating agencies but also with potential lenders. Even a one
per cent addition to the rate of interest paid on new borrowing would significantly increase the cost to Scotland. A
number of factors are important here – not least whether or
not Scotland has its own currency and whether, if it continues to use sterling, there is a credible lender of last resort.
These issues are dealt with in a later chapter. The consequence of all these reservations is that it would be unwise
to assume, in the event of Scotland becoming independent,
that its deficit would actually turn out to be as is given in
the GERS estimate. It could scarcely be lower but it might
easily be higher.

It would be wrong to leave this subject, however, without
considering what might happen in future under the present
arrangements, whether or not there is an enhanced degree
of devolution. Quite apart from the view expressed by the
Holtham Commission, there has been an increasingly strong
view in England that, under the Barnett formula arrangements, Scotland receives a more generous share of public
expenditure than is justified. Sooner or later this may lead
to some action by a future UK government. This is counter-
balanced by a fear in Scotland that, since the Barnett formula is only a population ratio, it will eventually result in
the squeeze that was earlier expected. As already explained,
it is impossible to tell whether the present level of public expenditure, and in particular the extent to which it is above

the UK average, is justified in the absence of a proper needs assessment. So far, pressure to address this issue has been ignored, with the government saying it has no plans to alter the formula. But a time may well come when this line can no longer be sustained and a revised system is introduced that allocates expenditure more closely in relation to need. If that happens, it should be based on a full needs assessment across all the regions and countries of the UK and carried out by an independent body, acceptable both to the three devolved administrations and to the government of the UK. Scotland would very probably then find itself required to reduce its public spending. I have always taken the view that, sooner or later, this would be inevitable but that the adjustment should be planned over a long period and at a time when the economy was buoyant. It would clearly be painful and would have major political consequences if attempted in circumstances such as the present.

Actually, since Scotland's population is only about 8.4 per cent of the total population of the UK, a redistribution of spending between the four countries of the UK to accord with a needs assessment would make little difference to England and would scarcely be noticed by the average voter. But that would certainly not be the case in Scotland. It may be, therefore, that the present arrangements will endure for a considerable time, simply because the UK government might not think it worth the hassle of making a change or of incurring political problems in Scotland, when the constitutional issue is in the minds of the electorate.

What this means, however, is that, whether Scotland remains part of the UK under any scheme of devolution or becomes independent, there is likely to be pressure on its level of public spending. Independence would involve uncertainty both over the level and volatility of oil revenues, for which the prudent policy would suggest that relying on them to balance the budget should be avoided and a part of them at least paid into a special fund. Remaining a devolved part of the UK, on the other hand, is likely to mean that eventually the level of expenditure will have to be justified through a needs assessment. The crucial difference is that, as an independent state, Scotland would be entirely responsible for its budget from the time that it became independent and would have to live within its means. But, as parts of a larger state, the revenue and expenditure of the individual countries and regions that form the UK would not need to balance. With broadly comparable taxes, the richer areas would contribute more than those that were poorer and expenditure would not be related to the revenue of a particular country or region but to what is required to provide a comparable level of public services.

Devo-Max, Devo-Plus and the Status Quo

The independence debate has seen the publication of several schemes that could have formed the basis of a third option in the 2014 referendum to give greater devolution. It is commonly said that more devolution is what the majority of Scots would vote for, had the option been available. Indeed, an Ipos/MORI poll conducted in June 2012 found that 41 per cent of those responding favoured Scotland remaining part of the UK but with increased devolution, 29 per cent favoured Scotland remaining part of the UK with the same powers as at present and 27 per cent wanted Scotland to become a fully independent country. The referendum, however, will be a straight choice between independence and the status quo, with no third option.

What might such an option have amounted to? It is worth considering this, even if it is not an option in the referendum, because, in recognition of popular pressure, some members of all three unionist parties are working on options for greater devolution, which may lead to implementation after the referendum. At present, neither the details nor the implications of a third option are well understood; nor are many people yet fully aware of what the status quo would amount to because the Scotland Act 2012 has not yet taken effect and will take some time to do so. The status quo does not therefore mean continuing with devolution as it has been since 1999. That is no longer possible.

The Status Quo

If independence is rejected in the referendum and the UK government brings forward no further proposals to enhance devolution, the Scotland Act 2012 will form the basis of the system of government in Scotland. This will increase the powers of the Scottish Parliament as set out in the UK government's White Paper 'Strengthening Scotland's Future',[1] which closely followed the recommendations of the Calman Commission on Scottish devolution set up by the three unionist parties in the Scottish Parliament.[2]

Much of the Act is concerned with working arrangements between the two governments but the most important provisions, and those that concern us here, are those that are designed to give greater responsibility to the Scottish Parliament for raising revenue. It has been a major criticism of devolution since 1999 that the Scottish Parliament had responsibility for a large part of public expenditure in Scotland but very little for raising the revenue to finance it. That resulted, it was argued, in insufficient accountability for the spending decisions that Parliament made. Under the system that has applied since 1999, the only taxes for which there is any responsibility in Scotland are council tax and business rates. The Act setting up the Parliament gave power to vary the standard rate of Income Tax either up or down by 3 pence in the pound but this power was never used. As a result, only 14 per cent of expenditure for which responsibility lies in Scotland is financed by taxes set in Scotland.[3]

The principal change is that, in future, the Scottish Parliament will be required to set a Scottish rate of income tax each year to replace part of the UK income tax. From April 2016, the UK government will reduce the main UK rates of income tax in Scotland by 10 pence. The block grant will be reduced by a similar amount to compensate, leaving the

Scottish Parliament to determine what rate of income tax to levy, in place of the 10 pence, to finance its expenditure. Responsibility for the structure of tax rates will remain with Westminster but, if changes are made by the UK Parliament to the structure of income tax rates, a principle of 'no detriment' will apply. This would result in compensating changes to the block grant to ensure that Scottish government revenue is not affected.

This power over income tax represents a large flow of income – if the Scottish tax rate were 10 pence in the pound, it would raise £4,500 million or 17 per cent of the Scottish budget.[4] The Scottish rate of tax will apply to all those defined as Scottish taxpayers. This includes those resident in Scotland and those whose principal connection with the UK is with Scotland.

The Calman Commission found that the cost of applying the Scottish rate of tax to income from savings and distributions would be prohibitive and recommended instead that half of the tax revenue from this income should be assigned to the Scottish government. The White Paper accepts that applying the Scottish rate of tax to income from these sources is impractical but argues that assigning tax revenues does not enhance accountability. For this reason, neither assignment nor power to alter the rates on income from savings and distributions were included in the Act.

However, in addition to a share of income tax, the Act gives the Scottish Parliament complete responsibility for stamp duty tax on land and property (but not on documents or stock exchange transactions) and for tax on landfill. The revenue from these two taxes, however, is relatively modest compared with income tax. The Calman Commission recommended devolution of two further taxes – the tax on air passengers and that on aggregates. The revenue from them would also have been fairly modest but they are not included in the Scotland Act 2012; the former is presently being reviewed and the latter is subject to legal challenge in the European Courts. However, the Act also gives the Scottish government power to levy any new taxes, subject to approval by both the Scottish and UK Parliaments.

The effect of devolving the three taxes in the Scotland Act, together with the responsibility that already exists for council tax and business rates, is to increase to about 35 per cent the share of budget revenue for which the Scottish Parliament and local authorities would be responsible.[5] The White Paper argues that the revenue from these devolved taxes would finance a similar share of the Scottish government's budget to that of the devolved legislatures in Belgium, Italy, Spain and Australia.

In addition to these tax powers, the Act gives the Scottish Parliament substantial new powers to borrow. Under the arrangements that have applied since 1999, Scottish Ministers have had only limited power to borrow for short-term current spending and this power was never used. In future, because income from taxation is less predictable than from the UK block grant, the new arrangements involve a degree of risk that has not hitherto existed. To allow for temporary shortfalls resulting from this, as well as deviations between forecast revenues and expenditure, Scottish Ministers are to be given power to borrow up to £500 million for cumulative current debt. In addition, they will have power to borrow up to 10 per cent of the capital budget in any one year, with a limit of £2.2 billion on the total stock of borrowing for capital investment.[6]

This regime would reduce the share of public expenditure financed by the block grant to 65 per cent. At present, as Chapter 1 explained, this grant is determined by the Barnett formula and has attracted much criticism, especially in England. But, apart from reducing the share of public expenditure that it would finance, there are no proposals to change it.

While these changes in taxation and borrowing will increase the accountability of the Scottish Parliament, they do not do anything to give the Scottish Parliament power and responsibility over macroeconomic policy. Indeed, the White Paper explicitly reserves this to Westminster. That does not mean, of course, that the Scottish government cannot adopt policies that improve the performance of the economy. Ways in which Scotland's economic growth might be improved with the Scottish government's existing responsibilities are discussed in the next chapter. Suffice it to say here that those who look for some independence in macroeconomic policy must accept that responsibility over demand management through monetary, fiscal and exchange rate policies must inevitably rest with the state and, in Scotland's case, even with devolution, that state is still the UK.

Devo-Max

Devo-Max has never been very clearly defined but it presumably means almost total fiscal separation of Scotland from the rest of the UK. Contributions would still be required to meet the costs of common services such as the royal family, defence, servicing the national debt and foreign embassies; monetary union with the rest of the UK would continue and foreign exchange reserves would be held for the UK as a whole. The main feature of such an arrangement would be that there would be no social pact. If Scotland were wealthier than other parts of the UK, it would not be expected to contribute support to them and, if Scotland was poorer, it could not expect any help from them. No attempt would be made to equalise social provision, and welfare benefits, including State Pensions, might be at different rates from their equivalents elsewhere in the UK.

It is not easy to find examples of this kind of arrangement

in other countries. The Campbell Committee said it was not aware of any.[7] The case that seems to come nearest to it is that of the Basque country and Navarra in Spain and this is referred to by the Scottish government.[8] The Basque country has a higher GDP per head than the Spanish average and has a population of only 2 million, 5 per cent of the Spanish total. In a recent paper for the David Hume Institute, César Colino argued that this system has been profitable for the Basque country because of its relative wealth.[9] Unsurprisingly, it has attractions for the areas that are richer than the rest of the country but is considered unjust by the others.

Even here, however, there is not complete fiscal autonomy. In accordance with EU rules, there can be no separate rate of VAT and the Spanish state retains responsibilities for social security, justice, defence, foreign affairs, transfers to the EU, macroeconomic policy and regulation of the financial sector. A contribution for these central services is paid by the Basque country to the Spanish state. Indeed even with this large amount of devolution, 50 per cent of Basque public expenditure, mainly for State Pensions and unemployment benefits, remains the responsibility of the central government which also raises 40 per cent of the public revenues.[10] The Basque country therefore remains subject to fiscal decisions made by central government, including the policies to reduce the Spanish budget deficit. The Spanish government has also had to defend its fiscal arrangements for the Basque country against appeals from the European Commission at the European Court of Justice.

Could such a system work in Scotland? As was shown in the last chapter, public spending per head is some 10 per cent above the UK average, while revenues, excluding oil and gas, are no more than equal to the average. So, unless the Scottish government received a geographical share of oil and gas revenues, there would have to be some sharp cuts in public expenditure. The geographical share of North Sea revenue would approximately cover the higher level of spending but, so long as Scotland remained a part of the UK, the rest of the UK might see it as unreasonable to give Scotland so much of the North Sea revenue and resist any change. At present the offshore area is not divided between different countries in the UK but is treated as a resource for the benefit of the whole state. The UK government would probably want that to continue.

Under Devo-Max there could still be no separate rate of VAT and welfare and social security would be problematic (a discussion of welfare devolution is in Chapter 8). There could also be a strong political reaction from any part of the UK that felt it was disadvantaged by the financial arrangements for Scotland. Indeed, it could well be that, rather than accept such an arrangement, the rest of the UK might prefer to let Scotland become an independent state.

Some experts have argued that fiscal independence would encourage the Scottish government to put a greater emphasis on economic growth, so that its economy performed better. Professors Andrew Hughes Hallett and Drew Scott were subjected to close questioning on this by a committee of the Scottish Parliament in early 2011 after asserting that there was evidence of this from other parts of the world.[11] But the evidence is not very convincing and, in Scotland's case, politicians of all parties share a commitment to try to improve the country's rate of economic growth. If they were aware of measures that would improve the country's performance, they should already be adopting them.

Devo-Plus

Several suggestions have been put forward for giving Scotland more devolution than will be provided by the Scotland

Act 2012 but not going as far as Devo-Max. Indeed, there have been so many proposals that many people may find them confusing. The following paragraphs outline and discuss three such schemes from:

- an interparty group of Liberal Democrat, Labour and Conservative MSPs chaired by Jeremy Purvis and published by Reform Scotland;[12]
- a committee set up by the Liberal Democrats, chaired by Sir Menzies Campbell;[13]
- a report for the Institute of Public Policy Research (IPPR) by Professor Alan Trench.[14]

This last, which was only published as this chapter was being written, seeks to outline a system that could be applicable to all three devolved administrations in the UK and contains the most comprehensive discussion of what is possible. All of these see major advantage for Scotland in remaining part of the UK but consider that there is a case for additional fiscal powers to make devolution more acceptable. Both the Purvis group and the Campbell Committee would like the Scottish Parliament to be entrenched by legislation, so that it could only be dissolved if it agreed, and the UK Parliament's power to legislate on devolved matters removed. The Campbell Committee would see this as a step towards a proper federal constitution for the UK.

The Purvis group's proposals, which are in three stages, go much further than the others and raise some of the same difficulties as were noted with Devo-Max. All three sets of proposals include complete devolution of income tax but the Campbell Committee would retain the same system of allowances and reliefs throughout the UK and does not consider that taxation from savings and investments could be devolved. It suggests assignment of the revenue instead. Purvis proposes devolution of corporation tax by

2020, something the SNP Scottish government would also like; the Campbell Committee, on the other hand, do not consider it an appropriate tax to devolve; and Trench outlines the substantial difficulties for both companies and tax authorities. He refers to the dangers of companies shifting their profits to the part of the UK with the lowest tax and concludes that it would only be possible if profits were allocated between the constituent countries and regions of the UK on the basis of payroll.

Only the Purvis group proposes eventual devolution of a geographical share of North Sea revenues. The Campbell Committee argue that the whole of Britain's offshore area should be under a single regime and not divided, while Trench suggests that a population share of the revenues could be allocated to the Scottish government. None of the three propose devolution of VAT, as different rates of this tax within a single member state are not permitted under EU rules, but Trench suggests that the revenue (apart from the contribution that goes as revenue to the EU) could be assigned to the devolved administrations. None of the schemes propose devolving responsibility for national insurance. This accords with their views on welfare expenditure. Although the Purvis group would like the Scottish government to be given a larger role in welfare, all three accept that the bulk of welfare expenditure, including the State Pension, should remain with the UK government. In the end, taking account also of the other smaller taxes it wishes to see devolved, the Purvis group's proposals would result in almost all of the expenditure of the Scottish government and local authorities eventually being covered by taxes raised in Scotland. The other two sets of proposals would result in around 55 per cent being financed by taxes raised in Scotland; they would therefore need to be supplemented by a significant but smaller block grant.

Both the Campbell and Trench proposals recognise that the block grant, as determined by the Barnett formula, is no longer acceptable to the whole UK and that it should move to a system based on an assessment of need. This would still give Scotland a bigger grant than a straight equalisation of fiscal revenue, such as applies in some federal countries, but the adjustment would be likely to involve a significant cut. The assessment should be carried out for all four countries of the UK and, ideally, for the English regions as well, and it is important that it should be done by an independent body in which all the administrations have confidence.

Assessment of Devo-Plus

How realistic are these proposals? It would certainly be possible to go beyond the changes made in the Scotland Act 2012. The Scottish Parliament could be made responsible for a greater share of income tax than the 10 pence envisaged under the Act. The case against this, as the Calman report argues, is that it could be unwise to have the Scottish government too heavily dependent on one tax, the proceeds of which could be volatile. Moreover, if the UK government had no locus at all in setting income tax in Scotland, it would have to rely on other taxes – particularly VAT – to provide for servicing the UK national debt, for defence and for dealing with emergencies such as arose in recent years to support the banks. Such expenditure could be substantial and subject to variation, as unexpected needs arise. These considerations point to some share of income tax remaining with the UK Parliament.

The Purvis group envisages the eventual devolution of fuel duty and excise duties but this is not proposed by the Campbell Committee and Trench only considers it for duties on alcohol and tobacco. But he shows there would be considerable difficulty even with them because they are levied not at the point of sale but of production or import. They would probably have to be replaced by a new tax altogether and, if it was a sales tax, that might conflict with EU rules on VAT. If the issue of accountability is a major concern, as I believe it to be, it would be possible to follow the practice in some other countries and assign the proceeds of VAT (as proposed by Trench) and some of the smaller taxes to the Scottish Parliament but without freedom to alter tax rates. Some people regard tax assignment as pointless if tax rates cannot be altered. But it would tie Scottish public expenditure more closely to the revenue actually generated in Scotland, enable the block grant to be much smaller and perhaps give less scope to taxpayers elsewhere in the UK to complain about unfair funding for Scotland. And, if the Scottish government was able through its policies to encourage the growth of the economy, some benefit from that would accrue to it through higher tax revenue.

Corporation tax is a contentious issue. The SNP government has made it plain that it would like this tax devolved.[15] There are a number of countries – Switzerland is an example – where corporate tax rates are set by the regions (in Switzerland's case, the Cantons). Following the judgment of the European Court of Justice in the Azores case, the EU only permits different rates of corporation tax within one member state if the region in which the tax is lower is not subsidised for this purpose by the rest of the state. Otherwise it would be regarded as a state aid and subject to the competition rules on state aids. The Holtham Commission on a funding settlement for Wales has proposed a rebate or a lower rate of tax where levels of GDP are well below the average of the state.[16] That would make it part of regional policy to encourage investment in poorer areas, even if it had to be financed by the region itself. Since Scotland's GDP per head is very close to the UK average, this would not apply, even if such a scheme were eventually implemented elsewhere in the UK.

In a UK context, I have always regarded devolution of corporation tax rates as raising major difficulties. The strongest case is that made for Northern Ireland, where it can be argued there is a competitive disadvantage because the standard rate of corporation tax in the neighbouring Irish Republic is only 12.5 per cent. The SNP government's desire to have control of this tax seems to stem from the Irish Republic's success in using it to attract inward investment but it has also resulted in companies simply basing their registered offices in Ireland (the so-called 'brass plate effect'). Even in such cases, of course, Ireland has still benefitted from tax on the revenue declared at the registered office.

If Scotland had ambitions to follow this example while still part of the UK, it would help to attract investment to Scotland so long as the difference in tax rates was substantial but much of this might be at the expense of other parts of the UK and would be particularly resented in Wales, the north of England or other regions, where GDP per head is lower than in Scotland. They would probably make a case for equal treatment. Even then, it could produce major distortions. For these reasons, I would expect it to be strongly resisted by the UK government. Moreover, the Scottish government already has power over business rates, which yield almost £2 billion a year and can be altered as it thinks fit. A lower rate of corporation tax would reduce revenue for the Scottish government, which Trench estimates at a loss of £1,724 million a year, if it were cut to the Irish Republic's rate. Unless it provided such a stimulus to the economy that it made up for the loss, this would be a problem for the government and, even if there was a significant stimulus, it would take years to make up for the lost revenue.

Oil and gas revenues were proposed for devolution by the Purvis group for the third stage of its scheme. But, as argued already in relation to Devo-Max, so long as Scotland remained part of the UK, there would be no formal need for any division of the offshore area and I suspect that the UK government would want to continue to treat it as a resource for the whole UK. I would therefore expect strong resistance from the UK government.

Conclusion

Devo-Max offers the opportunity for greater independence in economic policy but it would probably provoke major resistance from other parts of the UK. This would be especially so if policies were seen as unfair or discriminatory. But the important point about Devo-Max is that, like independence, it would end the social pact with the rest of the UK whereby there is pooling of resources to achieve equality of social provision. Scotland would also have serious difficulty in funding its above-average level of public expenditure unless it received the geographical share of tax revenues from the North Sea oil that it could expect as an independent state. Such terms seem unlikely to be acceptable to a UK government so long as Scotland was part of the UK. Differences in corporation tax and some other taxes as well as in levels of benefit would also create distortions and anomalies, which could provoke strong reaction from other parts of the UK. Devo-Max is an attempt to have complete financial independence, apart from monetary policy, while remaining in the UK. That is unprecedented elsewhere, even in the Basque country which comes closest to what the proponents of Devo-Max might want. For Scotland, if it were implemented, it would involve many of the risks of independence without either the UK safety net or the policy freedom of independence.

The Devo-Plus schemes all improve accountability. The proposals of the Purvis group raise some of the same difficulties as Devo-Max over the devolution of corporation tax and Scotland's geographical share of revenues from the North Sea. The proposals of the Campbell Committee and Alan Trench's report for IPPR, however, do not raise these problems and they seem to me to be workable. They would result in more of the Scottish government's public expenditure being financed by Scottish tax revenues and less by block grant than with the status quo after implementation of the 2012 Scotland Act.

Scottish Revenue in 2011–12 from Taxes Proposed for Devolution

	£million
Income tax (three quarters of total)	8,092
VAT (minus EU contribution)	9,269
Insurance premium tax	251
Aggregate levy	52
Landfill tax	97
Stamp duty land tax	275
Air passenger duty	213
Council tax	1,987
Business rates	1,933
Total	22,169
Total Scottish government and local authority expenditure	38,624
Taxation revenue as a % of expenditure	57.4

Source: Government Expenditure and Revenue Scotland 2011–12, *March 2013*

The table above sets out a suggested scheme for increased devolution of taxes that seems to me realistic and would have a chance of being acceptable. It builds on the Devo-Plus proposals of the Campbell Committee and Alan Trench but does not accept all their suggestions. The main difference is that only three quarters of income tax revenue would be devolved, on the grounds that to cope with unexpected demands and emergencies the UK government should retain some power to levy such a major tax. This introduces a complication, however, because if a Scottish government wanted to alter the structure of income tax, which I think it should have power to do, the UK component would have to be separated and possibly form a separate tax. This would be necessary if the Scottish government had a different view from the UK government over which group in society should bear the greatest tax burden. I would assign the revenue of VAT, subject only to the deduction for the required funding for the EU, while accepting that there would be no power to alter rates. This is because I attach importance to making revenue from taxes in Scotland cover as much of public expenditure as practicable. It would also enable the Scottish government to benefit from any increased revenue as a result of improved economic performance.

Together with the other smaller taxes in the Scotland Act and the air passenger duty and aggregates levy, which were proposed by Calman but not so far implemented, the revenue from these taxes would cover over half the expenditure of the Scottish government and local authorities; the block grant would be substantially reduced and what remained would have to be gradually adjusted to accord with a proper needs assessment. Such an assessment, however, should be undertaken for all the countries and regions of the UK to ensure that the distribution of expenditure between them was fair; and moving to it should be in accordance with a timetable agreed by all three devolved administrations and the government of the UK.

In considering the various options outlined in this chapter, it is important to be clear what the purpose of more devolution is. All of the schemes discussed would result in a greater part of Scottish public expenditure being financed by taxes raised in Scotland. But what is it that the advocates of more devolution actually want? Probably more control over the policies that are applied to Scotland; and, while the increased tax-raising powers under these schemes make possible a somewhat different spread of taxation according to income, they do not perhaps do as much to make possible the substantial differences in policy that some people may wish. The scope for increased control that independence would give is discussed in the next chapter.

3

The Scope for an Independent
Economic Policy

The last chapter discussed the scope for greater economic powers for the Scottish Parliament under various schemes for devolution. These could result in Scotland raising more of its own tax revenue, thereby resulting in increased accountability, but the scope for independence in managing the economy would be limited. This is especially so as fiscal, monetary and exchange rate policies would all be reserved to the UK government. Schemes for greater devolution might give the Scottish government greater power to borrow than it has now and there could be some differences in income tax rates and other devolved taxes. But the essence of macroeconomic policy is the ability to budget for a surplus or a deficit, so as to control inflation and stimulate economic growth. Policy to deal with these matters would inevitably remain with the UK government.

With independence these constraints theoretically disappear and Scottish Ministers have claimed that only independence would give them the levers they need to manage the economy in the interests of the Scottish people. But, in practical terms, no government can pursue policies regardless of what its neighbours and trading partners are doing. All economies nowadays are interdependent, as can readily be seen from the effect on the UK of policies in the United States and the European Union. This would be especially so for Scotland, given its relatively small size, the fact that the rest of the UK would be its dominant trading partner and that freedom of movement of both capital and labour throughout the single market of the present UK would continue.

Fiscal Policy

An independent Scotland would raise all of its own tax revenue, including personal taxation, VAT, excise duties and corporation tax; it would have to decide what rates should be set for each tax. It would also be responsible for all of its public expenditure, including defence, foreign embassies and interest on the national debt, items that are at present dealt with centrally by the UK.

But there would still be constraints. Differences in VAT or in excise duties, although allowed for individual states under EU rules, could encourage trading across the border, if they were substantial, as happens now with alcohol between Britain and Continental countries. If personal taxation was different from the rest of the UK, there would be a risk that some people would vote with their feet and move either to or from Scotland, though I suspect that the difference would have to be significant, certainly larger than present differences in council tax, for this to become an issue. The UK is not only a single market for goods and capital but the integration of the labour market also makes it very easy for people to move to wherever gives them most opportunity. Obviously there is no language barrier as applies between other EU countries.

Differences in rates of corporation tax exist between EU countries. But, if the Scottish government tried, as is its stated aim,[1] to reduce the rate of tax to a very low level, it could be seen as an attempt not just to help companies in

Scotland but to attract economic activity that might otherwise go elsewhere in the UK or to other member states of the EU. That would raise problems both with the European Union and the remainder of the UK. As it is, several EU countries have taken issue with Ireland's low 12.5 per cent rate of corporation tax, notably at the time of the Irish financial bailout, arguing that it was unacceptably distorting. While Ireland has, so far, managed to resist this pressure, it is unlikely that a newly independent Scotland, seeking to establish itself within the EU, would be able to do so.

Moreover, as a response to the difficulties in the eurozone, proposals are being developed that would include a banking union and much greater integration of fiscal policy for countries in the zone. This will apparently give members of the zone some oversight of each other's budgets, with the intention of ensuring that they all pursue policies of financial rectitude. It is not clear at present how far this will go or whether it will be acceptable to member states. But it is likely to increase pressure for greater harmonisation of taxes, including corporation tax, even for countries that are not in the eurozone but are part of the EU.

The Importance of North Sea Oil Revenues

The inclusion of the North Sea on a geographical basis makes a substantial difference to the size of the Scottish economy. As we have seen in Chapter 1, it would immediately add about 21 per cent to Scotland's GDP.[2] It would also provide a large flow of taxation revenue and such revenue would be a much larger component of a Scottish government's budget than it has been of the budget of the UK. Its contribution to the balance of payments would also be very important and, if there were a separate Scottish currency, its value would be heavily influenced by the price and volume of oil produced. The problem, as we also saw in Chapter 1, is that the value of the oil and gas produced has fluctuated over the years, not just because output has varied but even more because prices have been volatile.

The implications of North Sea oil revenues for the balance of payments and the exchange rate are considerable and could be the opposite of those for the government's budget. The higher the revenues, the more the Scottish government's budget would gain. But the balance of payments on foreign transactions is a different matter. There are no estimates of what Scotland's balance of payments, in the event of independence, might be. But a high oil price and, consequently, high revenues carry the danger that, by generating a large balance of payments surplus, they could push the exchange rate up, if Scotland had its own currency, thereby threatening damage to the non-oil economy. This is not a minor concern. The Dutch economy suffered in the 1970s when discoveries of natural gas threatened to damage non-gas related activities and this became known as 'the Dutch disease'. In the same way, the massive growth in UK oil revenues in the early 1980s was one of the factors that brought about a very sharp rise in the sterling exchange rate, which, in turn, was a major factor in the recession of those years and caused the loss of a lot of manufacturing industry.* The Scottish government would therefore have to stand ready to counteract this effect by investing abroad, as Norway has done with its oil fund, or by some other means, if the rest of the economy was being affected.

As part of the UK, Scotland has been within a state where revenue and expenditure in the individual territories and regions did not need to balance, as explained in Chapter 1. Policy has been based on the assumption that the stronger

---

* This effect was, of course, compounded by the very tight monetary policy adopted by the UK government in the early 1980s.

parts of the country help the weaker, thereby enabling a comparable standard of public services to be maintained, which some of them would otherwise be unable to afford.

There have also been centrally funded regional development policies to help growth in areas in need of development or to replace activities that have declined. Such policies have varied greatly in strength, depending on the philosophy of the government of the time. But Scotland has, over the last half century at least, been one of the parts of the UK that has benefitted. Within federal states, similar transfer mechanisms and development policies usually exist. The Scottish electorate would therefore have to decide whether it wanted to retain the safety net of being part of a larger country, where there is a generally comparable standard of public services, regardless of what can be afforded from local taxation at any particular time or whether, for the sake of being independent, it will take the risk that there may be times when, perhaps because of a drop in oil revenues or some other reason, taxation revenue falls and public expenditure has to be cut to match it. Those arguing for independence or some form of complete fiscal autonomy for Scotland, such as Devo-Max, need to face up to this issue, as their policies would end such inter-regional transfers.

Monetary Policy and the Choice of Currency

The Scottish government has said that it would be its intention to keep sterling as the national currency following independence and that the monetary union of the UK would therefore continue. This is also the recommendation of the 2013 report of the Scottish government's Fiscal Commission.[3] But this leaves a host of important questions unanswered. Would the Scottish government sell its own bonds on the market and, if so, what interest rate might they have to pay? How much influence would the Scottish government have on the Bank of England's monetary policy? On what conditions would the Bank of England be prepared to continue as lender of last resort for Scotland? It would seem that no discussions about this with the Bank have so far taken place. If the Scottish government wanted it to perform this role, the Bank's agreement and that of the government of the remainder of the UK would have to be sought. A Scottish request for continued Bank of England support as lender of last resort could meet with refusal, especially if the remainder of the UK was not satisfied with the economic policies being followed by Holyrood.

If agreement was reached to enable the Bank of England to act as a central bank for both countries, it might be possible, following the example of the European Central Bank (ECB), to argue for there to be a Scottish member of the Court of the Bank. Scottish Ministers have said they would want Scottish representation on the Bank's Monetary Policy Committee (MPC). That is likely to be more difficult and, again, it might be refused. None of the present members of the MPC or the Court is there to represent a particular territory. If Scotland and the rest of the UK were in monetary union, there might be a Scottish member of the MPC but only so long as he or she had appropriate expertise and was not there just to represent the interests of Scotland. And, as the example of European monetary union shows, even representation on the board of the ECB does not guarantee a monetary policy that suits all members; inevitably the largest economies are those to which the bank has to pay most regard in deciding its policy. In Scotland's case, there would be a huge demographic imbalance with the remainder of the UK having over 91 per cent of the population. Scotland's influence would therefore be bound to be limited.

Alternatively, within the monetary union, might there

be a Scottish central bank? If so, would it then be able to act as lender of last resort? This might depend on whether Scotland continued to use Bank of England notes or re-established the separate pound Scots, which could be pegged to be exchangeable at par with sterling. If the European example is a guide, within EMU the individual central banks of member states do not have money-creation powers and therefore cannot act as lenders of last resort for their respective countries. Had they retained their own currencies but linked them to the euro, they might have been able to do so but, depending on the circumstances, their actions could then put the currency link under great pressure, eventually forcing it to break to form a new exchange rate. This is what happened with the regime of fixed exchange rates in the European Exchange Rate Mechanism (ERM), in the years when it preceded the single currency.

Here the experience of Ireland is interesting, although the present circumstances of Scotland and those of the then Irish Free State in 1922 are very different. After independence, Ireland retained sterling as its currency and conditions were much as they are in Scotland now – Bank of England notes continued to circulate and the Irish banks issued notes of their own, which were accepted as sterling both by businesses and members of the public and were backed by deposits at the Bank of England. The first Irish Banking Commission set up in 1926 proposed introducing Ireland's own currency notes but emphasised the importance of retaining the 1:1 parity with sterling. These notes were therefore exchangeable at par with Bank of England notes and managed by an Irish Currency Commission. In 1934, there was a second Banking Commission, one of the main recommendations of which was the establishment of a central bank. But Ireland did not actually get a central bank until 1943, following the Central Bank Act of 1942. The remarkable consequence of all this was that, in the absence of any formal agreement with the Bank of England, Ireland was without a lender of last resort for some 21 years. This is particularly surprising, considering that those years included the 1930s depression and the first four years of a world war.

Mercifully, this need did not arise as no Irish banks got into trouble during this time and successive governments operated extremely conservative fiscal policies. With much greater speculative activity now a feature of financial markets, it is hard to see an independent Scotland getting away with having no lender of last resort. Nor, one imagines, would an independent Scotland, trying to stimulate its economy and wanting to use fiscal levers for this purpose, be content with an extremely conservative fiscal policy of the kind followed by Ireland after independence. But, with a deficit of 5.0 per cent of GDP in 2011–12 (even including a geographical share of North Sea revenues), there would hardly be scope for an expansionary fiscal policy.

Was Ireland right to follow this policy of retaining the link with sterling through thick and thin? Successive experts, including the First Banking Commission and the majority report of the Second, argued strongly for this. But the minority report of the Second Commission disagreed, saying that they could not:

> acquiesce in the extraordinary view that this country, alone among responsible entities in the world, should not ever have the power to make decisions, and that no apparatus or mechanism for controlling the volume and direction of credit should ever be brought into existence.[4]

Nowadays there are some in Ireland who strongly criticise the policies pursued in the early decades after its independence. Conor McCabe, for example, argues forcefully that, given the poor and underdeveloped state of the Irish economy at that time, retaining an overvalued currency, which is what the parity link with sterling implied, was profoundly damaging to the economy and was one of the factors that led to Ireland's relative stagnation during that time.[5]

What is clear is that, if an independent Scotland wished to continue to use sterling, there would have to be negotiations with the rest of the UK and the outcome of these negotiations would be crucial to how policy operated. If the Scottish government wanted to borrow using common sterling bonds, like the eurobonds proposed but not yet implemented for the EU, that would imply that they were guaranteed by both the UK and Scottish governments. For this to be acceptable, the rest of the UK and Scotland would have to be satisfied on the sustainability of each other's fiscal policy, just as eurozone countries now see the need for fiscal union to support their monetary union. If, on the other hand, Scotland issued its own bonds to cover any necessary borrowing, these might require a higher interest rate than the bonds of the rest of the UK, until the market was satisfied, as a result of experience, that they were equally safe and fully backed by a lender of last resort.

So there is much that would need to be decided and many issues that have not as yet even been discussed. If Scotland does decide to become independent, my own view is that it, like Ireland after 1922, could continue in monetary union with the rest of the UK, if it accepted all the constraints that implied. But these constraints would be considerable, even if the UK government and the Bank of England were receptive to what Scotland wanted. Scotland would have very little influence on monetary policy and fiscal policy would, in effect, be overseen by the rest of the UK.

It is interesting to note that, when the Czech and the Slovak Republics split in 1993, before they joined the EU, they intended to maintain monetary union and a common currency at least initially, though with the prospect that they might adopt their own separate currencies eventually. In the event, the monetary union collapsed in less than six weeks, as a large volume of funds flowed from Slovakia into banks in the Czech Republic. Controls on capital movements had to be imposed and the existing Czechoslovak currency was over-stamped by each country to distinguish it, until two new currencies could be introduced. The lesson is that, if the markets think a monetary union will not last, it becomes very difficult and costly to maintain and will, in the end, fail.

Nevertheless, continuing the monetary union with the rest of the UK is the preferred policy of the SNP government and is probably how it would start, perhaps for some years. But it is likely that there would be a need for a separate central bank and, if Scotland was a member of the EU, this could be a required condition of its membership. A separate central bank would not mean the end of sterling monetary union – indeed, the eurozone countries all have their own central banks. But, if Scotland's central bank was to be given power to act as lender of last resort – and my view is that it should have such power – it would have to have a separate currency as well. This could be pegged to sterling or indeed the euro, depending on circumstances, just as monetary union continued with Ireland up to 1978. There would be considerable advantages in maintaining the sterling monetary union, as the Scottish government's Fiscal Commission argues, given the closely integrated nature of the Scottish economy with the rest of the present UK and the fact that some financial institutions based in Scotland do most of their business south of the border.[6] But, as Professor John Kay (formerly a member of the First Minister's Council of Economic Advisers) has recently said in a lecture at Glasgow University, the Scottish government's freedom of action to tailor policy to Scottish needs – the economic levers about which politicians so frequently speak – would be so constrained that it might, in the end, induce a Scottish government to create a separate currency.[7]

The importance of having a separate note issue, even if pegged to sterling, is that it would make it possible to avoid the type of disaster – stemming from loss of competitiveness – that has affected the countries of southern Europe within the eurozone. Some smaller countries in Europe that still have their own currencies, Denmark being one obvious example, have found that it makes sense to shadow the currency of a larger area, usually the euro. But this still gives them freedom, in extremis, to allow their currencies to be revalued either up or down, should the need arise. They are not locked into a monetary union from which they cannot escape. This may mean that interest rates are slightly higher than for the currency that is being shadowed, because of exchange rate risk, but the kinds of problems that are now so distressingly evident in Spain, Portugal, Italy and Greece could be avoided or at least substantially mitigated.

So there would be important decisions to be taken on the currency and on how a Scottish government would intend to manage its budget. We need a clearer statement from the government about the additional levers it seeks and how it would use them.

Economic Policy with Existing Powers

The truth is that there is much that the Scottish government can do with its existing powers to improve the growth of the economy. Assistance for economic development, education and skill training, and infrastructure investment are devolved responsibilities. All of these are of the greatest importance for the performance of the economy.

Vocational skill training has, in my view, always been treated as the poor relation of university education and has tended to suffer in consequence, not only in Scotland but in the UK as a whole. Increasing the number of university graduates is important for the economy and is to be greatly welcomed, but the economy also depends on a good supply of school leavers who acquire high quality vocational skills. There seems now to be a tendency to regard qualification in vocational skills as in some ways less important or second best. The Scottish government recently decided to reduce funding for further education colleges while, at the same time, adhering to the policy of free university education for Scottish students at Scottish universities, despite the decisions of the other countries in the UK to charge fees. This decision has raised doubts over whether Holyrood has thought through its priorities on higher education properly.

When compared with some other parts of the UK, an important feature of the Scottish economy has been the relatively poor growth from new business start-ups and from small businesses. Scottish Enterprise and the SDA before it have given a lot of attention to trying to foster business start-ups and encouraging the growth of small firms. But it is not easy – a lot of small businesses fail and whether others succeed may depend heavily on the support they get. This was a large part of the rationale for setting up the SDA in 1975, with which I was then involved. It was believed at that time that there was a shortage of equity finance for small businesses. This, it was argued, made them too heavily dependent on bank finance in the form of loans and so gave them insufficient flexibility to survive fluctuations in the market.

There have been many improvements to the availability of equity finance since the SDA was set up. But, following the financial crisis of the last few years, funding from the banks has become much harder to obtain, as the priority for them has been to rebuild their balance sheets and increase their capital. This makes it all the more important that the Scottish government, probably through Scottish Enterprise and Highlands and Islands Enterprise, gives close attention to the needs of small businesses, both in the provision of advice and in meeting their financial needs.

Many entrepreneurs start businesses nowadays with an eye to an eventual exit, often taking the form of takeover by a larger group. There is nothing wrong with that – indeed, without it, there would be less business formation. What can be more problematic is the takeover of much larger, longer-established UK companies. Obviously there are times when a company is struggling and takeover by a competitor or a large firm is the only way to save the business. Or the company may be stagnating under current management and the shareholders take the view that a change in control is the way to avoid eventual decline. But there are many examples where there has been little or no economic advantage in a change of control. In the UK, the takeover of Cadbury's by the American firm Kraft in 2010 is a case where nothing was to be gained either for the firm or the country by the takeover. Sometimes, fear that they will be taken over prompts the management of a successful firm to try to take over others to prevent it being taken over itself. The clearest examples of this are the two Scottish banks. As Ray Perman's recent book on Bank of Scotland makes clear, the disastrous merger of Bank of Scotland with Halifax largely came about because the management felt they were at risk if they remained independent.[8] In the case of the Royal Bank also, though there were certainly other factors, fear of takeover was probably in the minds of the board in trying to make the bank a bigger and yet bigger business.

It is high time something was done about this. Norman

Tebbit, when UK Secretary of State for Trade and Industry in the 1980s, removed from the rules for appraising take-overs a clause that required the authorities to take into account regional implications. This was done after a successful defence of the Royal Bank's independence, when a merger was proposed with Standard Chartered Bank in 1981 and the Hongkong and Shanghai Banking Corporation put in a counter bid. In my view, the regional implications need to be restored to the appraisal of such takeovers, not only for Scotland but for other parts of the UK as well. If the Scottish economy is to prosper, companies headquartered in Scotland should be protected from aggressive takeovers carried out only for short-term gain or for the aggrandisement of management. The conclusion must surely be that takeovers are too easy and that, in some cases, they can be seriously damaging. But it is not easy to see how such a change in policy could be effective unless it was done for the UK rather than just for Scotland.

In respect of all the issues set out above – vocational training, support and finance for new and small businesses, and takeovers – the Scottish government could learn much from Germany. The German economy has the largest and strongest manufacturing sector in Europe; the training of apprentices is well organised and few school leavers are without either further education or training. The *Mittelstand*, the small and medium-sized business sector in Germany, has been an outstandingly important feature of the economy and it depends in large degree for its success on its close links with financial institutions. And a longer-term view on the part of both business and finance has resulted in the takeover frenzy that has been such a feature of Britain being much less evident in the German economy.

Could the Austerity of the Last Few Years Have Been Avoided?

What, I suspect, supporters of independence or much greater devolution would really like is a government that has the power to do things differently from the rest of the UK in ways that would improve the quality of their lives. The austerity policies of the present UK government are a case in point. These policies have been controversial and they have resulted in a lot of hardship and unemployment.

There can be no dispute about the need for a country to be able to live within its means over the longer term. Neither the UK nor Scotland is doing that at present, as can be seen from their unsustainable budget deficits and the consequent rise in the UK national debt (see Chapter 1). But political independence has not saved other countries from similar trouble.

I am among those who think that Chancellor George Osborne's policies have been misguided and needlessly harsh. He has failed to meet his targets either for eliminating the budget deficit before the next election or to have the national debt falling by then. Austerity is now to be extended well beyond the term of the present Westminster Parliament. All of this stems from the banking crisis of 2007/08 (I discuss the difficulties that Scotland might have had in handling that in Chapter 5). The problem now is how to get the country back to a position where it is living within its means.

To many people and, it seems, to some politicians, a government deficit is seen as analogous to an individual spending more than he or she earns. The only solution then is to reduce spending so that it no longer exceeds income. But, for a country, the analogy is misleading. Cutting public spending and raising taxes affect the level of activity in the economy. This causes unemployment and expenditure on benefits to rise and taxation revenue to fall. The policy will therefore only succeed if these secondary effects are smaller than the initial gain to the budget's balance from the cut in expenditure or higher taxes.

This is what economists call the fiscal multiplier. If the multiplier is low, the secondary effects will be modest and the attempt to get the budget back into balance by cutting expenditure or raising taxes will have a good chance of success. But, if the multiplier is high, the secondary effects will nullify much of what policy is trying to achieve and a downward spiral may develop. This is what seems to be happening now in certain eurozone countries and has happened to some extent in the UK.

It seems that there was a serious misjudgement over the size of the fiscal multiplier at the start. Initially, it was thought to be low (about 0.5, meaning that, for a 1 per cent cut in public expenditure or increased tax, there would be a half per cent reduction in GDP growth).[9] But that was based on research done in normal times and more recent research by the International Monetary Fund has concluded that the fiscal multiplier is now much higher (in the range 0.9–1.7).[10] This is because, in normal times, a tightening of fiscal policy can be offset by a relaxation in monetary policy. Also, the earlier calculation assumed that the policy was applied by one country in isolation. In present conditions, with Bank of England interest rates at their lowest ever level, monetary policy cannot be relaxed further and almost all of Europe and the United States are trying to cut their budget deficits simultaneously. As each country does this, imports from other countries are reduced and the consequence of so many countries attempting this together increases the depressive effect. Action taken to reduce the budget deficit has therefore had a much greater impact on growth than anticipated and this, in turn, makes it much more difficult to get the budget into balance.

In an important paper, Dawn Holland and Jonathan Portes of the National Institute for Economic and Social Research conclude that the poor growth performance of most EU countries, including the UK, during this recession can be attributed to the attempts at fiscal consolidation. This is because of the spill-over effects from one country to another of the action taken and the inability of monetary policy to compensate.[11] These negative effects have been larger than governments expected. They might have been less if policy had been aimed at measures with a lower multiplier. These might include an increase in income tax, rather than VAT, because it would have more impact on higher income groups, who do not spend so much of their income, and cuts in current public spending being at least partially offset by increased infrastructure investment that can yield a return. The most important lesson, perhaps, is that countries are now so interdependent and the spill-over effects from one country to another so great that the most effective policy would be a programme of actions carefully co-ordinated between countries. It might have resulted in higher borrowing in the short term but the ratio of national debt to GDP would have stopped rising sooner, as the economy's growth began to pick up.

What are the implications of all this for an independent Scotland? The fiscal multiplier is not the same for all countries. Small open economies, such as Scotland's, will have a lower multiplier than large more self-sufficient ones, because so much of the depressive effect of cuts in public spending or increases in taxes will hit imports. While the adverse effect on growth of trying to balance its budget would be relatively small for a Scottish government acting on its own, the spill-over effects from and to other countries would be very large. This conclusion is not very surprising. It means that what a Scottish government could do to stave off the adverse effects on its economy of an attempt by the UK and other countries to get their budgets into balance would be very limited. Inevitably the Scottish economy would be very dependent on policies adopted by its trading partners, whatever the constitutional arrangement. That does not leave a Scottish government powerless – it could still, for example, decide its own spending priorities – but its effectiveness would depend on how far it was able to influence others and agree on co-ordinated action.

4

Scotland and Europe

Scotland's position in Europe, if it becomes independent, has generated a lot of debate. The SNP government were clearly at fault in their original claim that Scotland would automatically remain a member of the EU. The First Minister gave the impression that his government had received legal advice on the issue but it then transpired it had no such advice. This was a shambles. The UK government, on the other hand, said that Scotland, as a newly independent state, would be outside the EU and would have to apply for membership in the same way as any other candidate state. This was confirmed by José Manuel Barroso, the president of the European Commission, in a letter to the House of Lords Economic Affairs Committee. Lord Kerr of Kinlochard, former head of the Foreign Office, Ambassador and UK Representative to the European Union, warned that Scotland might find it difficult to obtain the same terms and opt-outs that had been available to it as part of the UK.[1]

On the other hand, Sir David Edward, the distinguished Scottish former judge at the European Court of Justice, has taken the view that, as there is provision under article 50 of the Treaty of Lisbon for a member state to withdraw from the EU and provides for a process of negotiation and agreement in such circumstances, it would be contrary to the spirit of the Treaties to suddenly treat Scotland as outside the EU, if by popular referendum it chose to become a separate state.[2] If leaving the EU involves negotiation, then

Scotland's circumstance must also be the subject of negotiation during the period between the referendum vote and the moment when separation took effect. He goes on to argue that the key is the good faith of other member states (including the United Kingdom until the moment of separation). The result of negotiation could then be treaty amendment, rather than a new Accession Treaty.

At the time of writing, the UK government has just published the detailed opinion it has obtained from two distinguished experts in international law, Professors James Crawford of Cambridge and Alan Boyle of Edinburgh University.[3] They acknowledge Sir David's argument but think it more likely that Scotland would be treated much as any other state wanting accession, which would require a Treaty of Accession. There is no precedent in international law. No part of an existing member state has become independent before and then applied for membership in its own right. There is therefore no recognised procedure that meets the case. All these views are, however, those of experts and are based on experience.

I claim no legal expertise but I find Sir David's view persuasive. To argue otherwise would mean that, at the time of separation from the rest of the UK, all existing arrangements with the EU including, presumably, grants from the Structural Funds, the Common Agricultural Policy (CAP) payments, provision for Erasmus students and access in Scottish territorial waters for fishermen of other member states would suddenly end. That would not happen even to a country that wished to leave the EU. All are agreed, however, that negotiations would be necessary and that the agreement of all existing 27 member states (or 28, assuming Croatia joins in 2013) would be required. The main difference is in the time it might take and the extent of the upheaval. If Sir David is right, it might be accomplished quite quickly, within the two or more years between the referendum result and actual separation from the rest of the UK. But it would still require all the other member states to agree.

The issue is of major importance, especially for business. Many of the inward investment companies that decided to come to Scotland did so because they saw it as a good base from which to serve the large EU market. Scotland had what they needed – good sites for development, a supply of excellent labour, including graduates, and a dependable political and legal environment. Those that came from the United States and Japan also probably found it helpful that the language they needed was English, since that has become the international language for business. If, therefore, access from Scotland to the European single market were now to appear to be at risk, not only would it be hard to attract more investment from abroad, but companies already here might begin to think of moving elsewhere.

There are some who have argued that, if Scotland becomes independent, that would mean repealing the 1707 Act of Union and that Scotland and the rest of the UK would then be exactly in the same position as new states. They then assert that, if Scotland has to apply for EU membership as a new state, so would the remainder of the UK. This is given short shrift in the legal opinion. It would be Scotland's decision in a referendum to secede from the UK, not any decision taken by the electorate in the rest of the UK. The rest of the UK would therefore be the continuing state and would inherit all the treaties signed by it before Scotland seceded. It would, however, have to face some, *probably* slight, adjustment to its terms of EU membership on such matters as the number of MEPs and its budget rebate, as it would no longer be a country of 63 million people. Scotland would be the new state and would have to negotiate with the EU afresh to decide its conditions of membership. This would include its voting rights, its number of MEPs and whether or not it sought the same derogations as the UK.

As part of the UK, Scotland has been in the EU for 40 years and there is therefore no question that it satisfies the criteria for membership. However the UK has derogations from the EU treaties enabling it to exclude itself from joining the euro or the Schengen free borders area. Like the rest of the UK, Scotland has also shared in the budgetary rebate negotiated by Mrs Thatcher, as UK Prime Minister, at Fontainebleau in 1984.

Schengen

Securing an opt-out from the Schengen area seems likely to be the least difficult of these problems. The Schengen Agreement was originally independent of the EU but was absorbed into EU law by the Amsterdam Treaty of 1997. It requires members to abolish internal border controls with each other, while strengthening them with non-member states. Its provisions include a common policy on people seeking temporary entry and harmonisation of external border controls. There are cross border police and judicial co-operation. The area includes all EU states except the UK and Ireland, although implementation is not yet effective in some of the newer members that are not yet fully compliant – in Cyprus because of the dispute with the northern Turkish part of the island and in Romania and Bulgaria because of concern over anti-corruption measures and organised crime. However, the Schengen area also includes several countries that are not members of the EU: Norway and Iceland are members stemming from the Nordic Passport Union, which predated Schengen; Switzerland joined in 2008 and Liechtenstein in 2011; and there are no border controls with the three micro-states of Monaco, San Marino and Vatican City.

The UK did not join because, as an island, it argued that frontier controls were a better way to control illegal immigration than identity cards, residence permits and registration with the police, which apply in other countries. And Ireland is also outside the area because, since its independence from the UK in 1922, both countries have maintained a common passport-free travel area. How well the control of illegal immigration argument stands up in the light of the UK's experience is perhaps open to question; but, if joining the area involved introduction of identity cards, that is something that the UK, having abandoned a scheme to introduce them, would certainly continue to resist.

If Scotland became independent, it would presumably argue that, like Ireland, it was part of a common passport-free travel area with the rest of the UK, with which it also has a unified labour market. It would seem quite unreasonable for a derogation to be resisted when it has been given to the UK and Ireland. But, in the unlikely event that it became a problem, Scotland would then, if it joined the EU, have to install border controls on travel to and from England, a prospect that would alarm many people.

Joining the Euro

Under the Copenhagen criteria which define whether a country is eligible to join the European Union, membership presupposes the candidate country's ability to take on all the obligations of membership which include adherence to the aims of economic and monetary union (EMU). This would include eventually adopting the euro. However, before joining the euro, a state's legislation, for example in relation to its central bank, has to be compatible with EMU and it must also have achieved a high degree of sustainable convergence, as measured by four specified criteria:

- achievement of a high degree of price stability, with a rate of inflation close to that of the three best performing countries;
- a deficit on the government's budget at or less than 3 per cent of GDP and a debt ratio of less than 60 per cent of GDP or declining so that it is seen to be approaching that level;
- ability to keep to the normal exchange rate fluctuation margins of the European Monetary System (EMS) of which it would have to have been a member for two years;
- durability of convergence within the EMS, as shown by long-term interest rate levels.

There was a fair amount of fudging of these criteria when the eurozone was set up. Several countries, notably Italy and Belgium, did not meet the 60 per cent debt rule but were accepted because they argued that the ratio was falling. Some also had difficulty with the 3 per cent deficit criterion but argued that they had taken action that would enable them to meet it. Greece would not have been admitted if the true state of its finances had been understood.

If independence was achieved as a result of the 2014 referendum, Scotland clearly would not qualify then or, indeed, for some time. The budget deficit would have to be substantially less than its present level – estimated by the Scottish government at 8.1 per cent for 2010–11 and 5.0 per cent for 2011–12 (including North Sea revenues – see Chapter 1) and its debt ratio, depending on how it is apportioned with the rest of the UK, will certainly be over

60 per cent; indeed, it would probably be closer to 80 per cent. It could be argued, of course, that most of the existing members of EMU have debt ratios of more than 60 per cent as a result of the financial crisis and recession. But the UK does not belong to the European Monetary System. Scotland therefore would not qualify until it had been a member for two years, had at least shown convincing progress in meeting the deficit and debt criteria, had kept to the normal exchange rate fluctuation margins of the EMS and had proved durability of convergence as reflected in the long-term interest rate on its bonds.

No country can be forced or obliged to join the EMS system of managed exchange rates. When Sweden held a referendum, the result was against joining EMU. It has therefore not joined EMS. So long as this position is maintained it will not become a member of the eurozone, although it must have been expected that it would, in due course, do so when it signed its Treaty of Accession. No one can now force it to join against the expressed wish of its people, and to ask it to leave the EU in consequence of this would be absurd. The Czech Republic continues to use its own currency, although Slovakia, from which it separated before joining the EU, has joined the eurozone. As a result of the serious crisis affecting the zone over the last few years, it is probably now less likely that the Czech Republic will join EMU in the foreseeable future, although again it must have been expected to do so when it joined the EU.

To my mind the most important point is that the financial crisis, especially the extreme difficulties experienced by the southern European countries and by Ireland, must have changed perceptions considerably, whatever previous expectations and requirements may have been. Not only will this have made countries that are not yet in the eurozone less likely to want to join but, as they wrestle with the problems of the zone and work towards closer financial integration, including a banking union, the countries now in the zone must be less enthusiastic about admitting a newcomer, especially one like Scotland, where its two large banks have so catastrophically had to be rescued.

If an independent Scotland were to remain in monetary union with the rest of the UK, in accordance with present SNP government policy, that would in any case preclude Scotland joining EMU, unless the UK did so. That now seems a very distant prospect if it is a prospect at all. For all these reasons, I would not expect existing members to insist on Scotland adopting the euro as its currency if it seeks membership of the EU as a separate state. In the midst of the present major crisis, the long-term outlook for monetary union in Europe is not at all clear. But circumstances can easily change. My own view, as discussed in Chapter 3, is that Scotland, as an independent country, should eventually have its own currency and this could be pegged either to sterling or to the euro, depending on what seemed in the country's best interest.

An EU Banking Union

The UK, along with Sweden and the Czech Republic, has also opted not to participate in the proposed EU banking union, of which all other EU states (not only those in the eurozone) are expected to be members. So that could become an issue too. All of this is still at a very early stage but the participating countries will be required to hand over supervision of their banks to a European Banking Authority under the control of the European Central Bank. This is to be followed by a common means for winding up financial institutions in trouble and a financial backstop for dealing with a banking crisis. These latter arrangements are not yet agreed, but they follow logically from common supervision of the banks.

An independent Scotland would have to decide what it should do about this. If it retained sterling as its currency, it could not reasonably participate in the banking union, so long as the rest of the UK did not do so. But, if Scotland had its own currency, there could be a strong case for it participating, even if it did not join the eurozone, as it would give added protection in the event of a major crisis, such as has been experienced in the last few years.

Conclusion on Opt-outs

So the EU countries would be faced with something they have never faced before – a country which has separated from a member state, which does not intend to join the Schengen area or the eurozone, but intends to remain in monetary union with the rest of the member state from which it separated. How would that be regarded?

Some other member states, worried about the precedent it set for parts of their own territories that might want to split off and follow the Scottish example, might try to use negotiations over these derogations as an excuse to raise difficulties over Scottish membership. In particular, it now seems that Catalonia is to have an 'advisory' referendum on whether to secede from Spain; there is ongoing concern about a possible split in Belgium between Flanders and Wallonia; and there is also concern in Cyprus that the northern Turkish part might seek EU membership in its own right. It may seem unfair, if Scotland otherwise satisfies the criteria, but these other cases are relevant because they could affect the attitude of other EU governments to Scotland's position. The last French president promised that his country would have a referendum before there was any further enlargement of the EU. It could be argued, if necessary, that this would not apply since Scotland is already in the EU as part of the UK. The Spanish foreign minister has suggested that his country might object because of Spain's concern about Catalonia. So the position is unclear and much skilful negotiation might be needed. Any one of the existing member states could impose a veto.

If, however, these concerns can be satisfied and, especially as at present the Scots enjoy European citizenship, it should be possible to extend EU membership to an independent Scotland. There would have to be negotiations, and these would involve the rest of the UK as well, as the secession of Scotland would affect various aspects of its membership, such as voting rights and the number of members of the EU Parliament. But such negotiations might be completed quite speedily, perhaps even within two years from the referendum. Scotland might have to agree to some conditions that it does not particularly like but that would become clear in negotiation. Goodwill would be the key to success. It is a political rather than a legal issue.

However, it is conceivable that, if relations between the UK and other Member States were to deteriorate further as a result of the present UK government's desire to renegotiate the terms of membership, with the threat of an In/Out referendum, the atmosphere of negotiations as regards the future position of Scotland might be quite different, and favourable to Scottish membership, particularly if Scotland indicates its willingness to accept all existing rules and commitments.

The EU Rebate

The rebate was negotiated as a result of extreme pressure from Mrs Thatcher, when prime minister, because it appeared that the UK, under the rules that then applied, would contribute a disproportionate share of the revenue for the EU budget and far more than it would get back in payments. At that time, the greatest part of the budget, some 80 per cent, was spent on the Common Agricultural Policy and much of the revenue came from import duties, including on imported agricultural goods. Britain had a relatively small but efficient agriculture that did not qualify for large amounts of support but was a large food importer, especially from the Commonwealth. Since then, however, the EU budget has expanded; agricultural and other natural resource based support, including a small amount on fishing, is still the largest component of its expenditure but, at 48 per cent in 2011, is much less important than it was, and the structural funds for support to areas in need of development have become a second very important area of spending, amounting to 36 per cent of the total budget.[4]

On the revenue side, the bulk of the money now comes from a contribution based on gross national income (GNI).* In 2012, this is forecast to contribute 74 per cent of total revenue and the proportion has been steadily increasing, probably to ensure that the costs are not too high for the poorer countries.[5] There is also a VAT contribution, which has steadily reduced as the GNI contribution has increased – it now amounts to only 11 per cent of the total. The traditional own resources, principally from import duties, amount to 15 per cent. The contribution of each country is therefore more closely related to ability to pay than it was at the time Britain's rebate was started. There are nine coun-

---

* GNI is net of income paid and received from abroad. This is important as, although it has never been calculated for Scotland, it would certainly be lower than GDP, if GDP included Scotland's geographical share of the North Sea and the profits of all overseas companies operating both offshore and onshore in Scotland.

tries that contribute more to the EU budget than they get back in receipts (see table). The remaining 18 countries are net beneficiaries. These are the poorer countries, especially those in the eastern part of the EU – Poland for example is a major beneficiary – but including also Spain, Portugal and Greece. They contribute less, because their incomes are lower, but they are also major recipients, because of the importance to them of agriculture and their need for development.

Net Contributors to the EU Budget in 2011

	Gross Contribution million euros	Net Contribution million euros	Cost per head in euros
Denmark	2,448.3	975.2	174
Germany	23,127.1	10,994.1	134
France	19,612.2	6,449.9	99
Italy	16,078.0	6,492.1	107
Netherlands	5,868.9	3,804.6	228
Austria	2,688.7	812.9	97
Finland	1,955.2	662.2	123
Sweden	3,333.6	1,576.6	166
UK	13,825.0	7,255.2	115
UK without rebate	17,420.0	10,850.9	172

Source: European Commission, EU Budget 2011: Financial Report, Brussels 2012

Many countries consider the British rebate no longer justified, especially as Britain is one of the wealthiest countries in the EU. In 2005, it was reduced by 25 per cent but, in future budgetary negotiations, it can be expected that there will be pressure from other countries to end it altogether.

Indeed, they might use the occasion of a negotiation with Scotland to try to end it not just for Scotland but for the UK. It would, after all, be reasonable at least to adjust it for the remainder of the UK to take account of Scotland's secession. The amount of each country's net contribution varies by a surprising amount from year to year. According to the EU budget, in 2011 the UK rebate was 3.5 billion euros and, as the table shows, the gross contribution, allowing for the rebate, made by the UK was 13.8 billion euros.[6] This was less than that contributed by France – 19.6 billion euros – or Italy – 16.1 billion – countries with similar populations. Germany, with a larger population, makes the largest contribution – 23.1 billion euros. After receipts, the net figure for the UK is 7.3 billion euros – still less than Germany but more than the other countries. However, on a per head basis, the table shows that the UK contribution is now substantially less than that of the Netherlands, Denmark, Sweden, Finland or Germany. Without the rebate of 3.6 billion euros, the contribution, less receipts, in 2011 would be 10.9 billion euros – still slightly less than Germany – and, on a per head basis, without the rebate, this would still be less than Denmark or the Netherlands and only slightly more than Sweden.

Scotland would therefore find it very difficult to get a share of the rebate, if it was negotiating to become a member state of the EU in its own right. First, because the other countries would see the negotiations as an opportunity to end the rebate for at least part of what had been the UK. But, secondly, the case for the rebate would be less strong than for other parts of the UK. Scotland has had substantial support from the European Structural Funds for areas scheduled under regional policy. In addition, Scotland has a large agricultural area and much of it is classified as Less Favoured Area under the Common Agricultural Policy

(CAP), which qualifies for special assistance; it therefore receives a significant amount of support, though perhaps not as much as it should. The Royal Society of Edinburgh Inquiry that I chaired found that Scotland's receipts from the CAP, especially the amount received for environmental projects, was lower than for other countries and lower than we thought justified, mainly because the UK was anxious to restrain growth in the total EU budget.[7] This could perhaps be subject to negotiation in future. But, in view of what it would qualify to receive and the attitude of other member states, any notion that Scotland might be able to retain a share of the UK rebate must be dismissed. Scotland would be a net contributor because, although there are no GNI figures at present, we know that Scotland would be among the wealthier countries of the EU. But the net contribution per head, even without a rebate, would be very unlikely to be as high as for some other small countries, such as Denmark, Sweden and probably Finland.

Membership of the European Economic Area As an Alternative to the EU

As discussed earlier, if Scotland had problems negotiating membership of the EU, it seems more likely that this would be for political than legal reasons. But, if that were to happen or if the conditions attached to membership proved unacceptable, how serious a setback would this be?

If full membership of the EU was blocked, Scotland could apply for membership of the European Free Trade Area (EFTA), which would give it membership of the European Economic Area (EEA). The EEA countries have unrestricted access to the European single market but have to meet the rules of that market, just as EU members do, and also make contributions to the EU budget. Members

of the EEA include Norway, Liechtenstein and Iceland.*
Switzerland is not a member of the EEA but has bilateral
free trade arrangements with the EU. The main difference
between being a full member of the EU and being in the EEA
is that EEA countries have no representatives on the EU
Commission or Council and no members of the European
Parliament; they therefore have no influence on the policies
of the EU, although they are subject to them and to all the
single market rules, if they are to get unrestricted access to
the market. This disadvantage has been a major factor in
encouraging countries such as Sweden, Finland and Austria,
which were previously members of EFTA, to become full
EU members.

A major difference between the EU and the EEA countries is that the Common Agricultural and Fisheries Policies
do not apply to the EEA. This has been a significant factor
in the decision of the Norwegian public to reject EU membership twice in referenda. Fishing is an important industry
for Norway, which, although sharing part of the North Sea
with EU states, also has its own continental shelf. Its agriculture faces major handicaps of climate and topography
and is therefore more highly protected than it would be under the CAP. These considerations, especially for fishing,
are also relevant to Iceland. Exclusion from the CAP would
mean that Scotland would have to finance all of its agricultural support itself, and such support would certainly be
needed, especially in the hill areas and the islands, if agriculture was to remain viable there.[8]

Exclusion from the Common Fisheries Policy (CFP) might
seem more attractive to many people, as it is commonly asserted that the policy has been too centralised, generally

---

* Iceland has applied for full membership of the EU. But in view of the importance to it of its fishing industry and its experience in the financial crisis, there
are important issues to be considered.

unsatisfactory for Scotland and has led to depletion of fish stocks. But the main problem with fisheries policy is that the efficiency of modern fishing boats has steadily increased to the point at which their ability to catch fish greatly out strips the supply of fish in the sea.[9] This is what has caused stocks to become seriously depleted. In an attempt to restrain overfishing, the EU has imposed catch quotas. But, in each year's negotiations at Brussels, Ministers (including Scottish Ministers) are pressed by their country's fishing industries, concerned understandably about their livelihoods, to get the best deal they can. This has meant that the quotas are usually higher than the scientific advice recommends.

Because many people in Scotland regard the CFP as a wasteful failure, there are those who would like to see responsibility repatriated. It is sometimes suggested that this should be one of the subjects in the Prime Minister's proposed renegotiation of the UK's relationship with the EU. The policy certainly needs to become less centralised and some moves to achieve that have already been implemented.[10] It has recently been announced that the practice of discards, whereby substantial quantities of fish are discarded at sea because they are over the allowed quota, is to end. This is very welcome and long overdue.

The main difficulty in getting reform is that not all of the fishing nations agree on what should be done. The North Sea, by its nature and geography, is a shared resource between all of the countries with a coastline bordering it. That is how the CFP operates and each country has a quota. If there were not a common policy, major problems would arise if each country tried to operate its own exclusive zone. Fish do not respect international boundaries, so that, to avoid overfishing, some means of limiting the amount of fish caught would have to be applied to all countries sharing that resource. Negotiations to achieve this would be complex and difficult and it is by no means clear that any resulting policy would serve Scotland better.

What if the UK Leaves the EU?

Overhanging any discussion of Scotland's future in the EU is, of course, uncertainty about the position of the whole UK. Prime Minister David Cameron has said that, if re-elected, he would intend to renegotiate the terms of UK membership during the next UK Parliament and then put the issue to the country in an in/out referendum on Britain's membership. Judging by the attitude of many Conservative backbenchers and some of the polls, the whole country could be heading towards the exit. The UK's constant ambivalence in its attitude to the EU is trying the patience of other member states and they might not now do much to resist the UK's departure. This does not bode well for a good outcome in a renegotiation.

There can be no doubt, however, that the way in which the EU is operating at present is unsatisfactory. Much of this is the result of extending institutions that were originally designed for six member countries to the enlarged EU of 27. Decisions take too long and are often very difficult, as has been very obvious during the eurozone crisis. Much of the irritation with the EU in Britain, however, stems from the rules for the single market, which seem to many people excessively bureaucratic; this is ironic because the single market has been strongly supported by British governments of both parties. Indeed, the 1992 Programme as part of the European Single Act was the brainchild of a British EU Commissioner, Lord Cockfield. It requires rules on standards, which can often be complicated, if member countries are to freely admit each other's goods. Otherwise non-tariff barriers, such as differing safety standards, could be a major obstacle to trade. But the irritation, if understandable, is increased by much of the Euro-sceptic press. It has gained strength in England and can be seen as a form of English nationalism, since it also has a great deal to do with concern over issues of sovereignty.

Whether it is true, as is commonly asserted, that Scotland is less Euro-sceptic than England is not really clear. Some polls have given results that appear to support this. Because of our history, there probably is less concern about sovereignty in Scotland, which lost much of its sovereignty in 1707, than in England, where it is a relatively new concept. But whether this would result in Scotland voting one way in an in/out referendum and England the other is far from certain. I suspect that, if such a referendum is eventually held, the disadvantages of leaving the EU and losing influence over so many policies that affect us would become much clearer and might well result in a decision by the UK to continue membership.

The EU will inevitably change, however, if the members of the eurozone proceed down the path of much closer fiscal and political integration, as seems at present to be the intention. Whether formally recognised or not, that would lead to a two-tier EU, with the members of the eurozone forming an inner core and the other countries, of which the UK is likely to be one, in an outer free-trading periphery. Some of the countries not presently in the euro might aspire to join but equally some of those at present using the single currency might, in the end, decide that the degree of integration envisaged involves a greater loss of sovereignty than they can accept and leave to join the periphery. Recognition of a proper two-tier EU is perhaps inevitable in the end and might make it easier for it to operate effectively, as suggested in some of the proposals for reform.[11]

If Scotland became independent and was accepted as a

member of the EU, I would expect it to remain outside the eurozone, for all the reasons already discussed, so that it would be in the outer tier, if there were one. It would not be sensible to try to become a member of the eurozone, so long as it was unclear whether inflation in Scotland could be kept at a rate that was compatible with other countries, especially Germany. Failure to do this would result in the economy becoming increasingly uncompetitive and it is because this has happened in several of its members that the eurozone is in its present difficulties. It must also be doubtful if Scotland, having become independent, would want to surrender the amount of sovereignty that would be expected of a member of the eurozone.

The really interesting question would be what Scotland's attitude might be if the rest of the UK voted in a referendum to leave the EU but Scotland's population voted to stay in. If there is a UK referendum, it will not be before the next UK Parliament and therefore after the Scottish referendum. Scotland's decision will therefore have been made. But, if, in advance of the Scottish referendum, it seemed likely that the UK was going to leave the EU, that could become a factor in the referendum debate. Those who regard continued EU membership as important and in the best interests of Scotland and its economy might then be more likely to favour independence.

Could an Independent Scotland Have Handled the Failure of the Banks?

The bank crisis of 2008 has done immense damage to the British economy and the consequences have been long lasting. At the time of writing, we are still struggling with its effects and it looks as if it will be a long time yet before a satisfactory rate of growth returns to the economy and the legacy of debt is overcome.

It was particularly distressing to those of us living in Scotland that it was Royal Bank of Scotland and Halifax Bank of Scotland (HBOS) that were in the worst state and had to be bailed out by government. Royal Bank is a Scottish bank with headquarters in Edinburgh. It was founded in the 18th century partly, it is said, because of concern that Bank of Scotland was too sympathetic to the Jacobite cause. Bank of Scotland dated from 1695 – before the Act of Union – and had a very proud history. It was the oldest bank in Britain, apart from the Bank of England, which was one year older. As an independent bank, it had enjoyed a reputation for good cautious management and strong growth but had merged with Halifax, the largest of the former building societies, to form HBOS in 2001. Although technically a merger, rather than a takeover, Halifax was by far the larger partner and most of the combined management team including the Chief Executive, James Crosby, and his successor, Andy Hornby, were from Halifax. Bank of Scotland had secured agreement, however, that the headquarters of the combined bank would be at The Mound in Edinburgh.

What happened at the Royal Bank would seem to be mainly due to megalomania on the part of the chief executive, Fred Goodwin, who dominated the management team. The directors too must share some of the blame. The bank had mounted a successful takeover of the much larger English bank, NatWest, outgunning a rival bid from Bank of Scotland, which had started the process. The takeover of NatWest had been a success and had been well conducted so that it yielded considerable savings. It had also extended its business worldwide, with takeovers in other countries, and built a huge new head office at Gogar on the outskirts of Edinburgh. It should have stopped there. It had quite enough to digest and, had it done so, it might not have had to be rescued or at least it would not have required the amount of help that was eventually necessary.

But, in October 2007, with a recession in the offing, together with Santander and Fortis, it launched a joint bid for the Dutch bank ABN AMRO, the largest ever bank takeover. This was a disaster both for Royal Bank and for Fortis. ABN AMRO proved to be toxic with many bad loans, which would never be repaid; and a key component, desired by the Royal Bank, was removed from the transaction before the sale. Coupled with the onset of the recession and the problems of excessive lending that affected almost all banks, Royal Bank had engaged in unduly aggressive and high-risk organic growth. The chief executive had pressed for balance sheet growth and the commercial, corporate and investment banking teams were given incentives to deliver this. This pressure for growth and incentives to achieve it resulted in some bad deals rather than careful assessment of risk. All of this brought the bank to the point of insolvency so that it had to be rescued with a £40 billion injection of taxpayers' money from government. So Royal Bank, which had briefly been the largest bank in the world, with outstanding loans exceeding, by 40 per cent, not just the Scottish but the UK GDP, became semi-nationalised. The government injected capital by taking a 60 per cent shareholding, which later had to be raised to 80 per cent, when more funds were required.

Bank of Scotland's merger with Halifax in 2001 came about for two reasons, which are well explained in Ray Perman's recent book.[1] The Bank could claim to have had the most successful record of all British banks, both in terms of growth and return on shares. But, following financial globalisation and the free-for-all climate that was the product of the government's 'Big Bang' in the 1980s, which ended the previous regulatory restrictions, it felt vulnerable to takeover because of its relatively small size. Maybe it was less of a takeover target than it imagined, as it would have been hard for any other management to run it better or to generate substantial savings. But it felt that to survive it had to grow. The problem was that, although it could increase the size of its loan book, it could not get its deposit base to grow sufficiently to support it without having to rely on wholesale finance from elsewhere in the sector. Originally banks had based all of their lending on their deposits. And, had they continued to do that, there would have been no banking crisis. But the Big Bang in Britain and the repeal of the Glass-Steagall Act in the United States had meant that retail banks could move into investment activities that had hitherto been the province of merchant banks in Britain or investment banks in the United States. This was not a feature of Bank of Scotland or HBOS. It was a much riskier activity but potentially also much more profitable than retail banking and it made takeovers in the banking sector much easier and more likely – hence what Bank of Scotland management saw as a threat.

To help it to grow, without being too dependent on wholesale finance, Bank of Scotland first attempted a merger with the former building society, Abbey National. This proved abortive when it was impossible to agree terms. The irony is that had the Bank only waited, it could have taken over Abbey National with a hostile bid on its own terms, as it was not long before the latter got into trouble. Instead, Abbey was taken over by Santander. However, having failed in its bid for NatWest and also in its attempted merger with Abbey National, the Bank felt that it had become exposed and that the chances that it would itself be the subject of a takeover had increased. Accordingly, when the possibility of a merger with Halifax arose, it seemed attractive. Halifax had demutualised to become a bank. It had a huge mortgage book, with about a third of the total mortgages in the UK, and this seemed to Bank of Scotland to offer a deposit base on which profitable lending could be increased.

Looking back with the benefit of hindsight at what happened to the world's banking sector in the period before 2008, some of what was done then seems hard to credit. How could institutions, whose credibility was based on their sound judgement in handling people's money, have got into such a mess? But, as with previous financial bubbles, few people saw it coming or had any understanding of the danger they were in. The securitisation of mortgages, whereby lenders, instead of keeping outstanding mortgages on their books as assets, had been able to divide them, package them and sell them on the world market as bonds, had made possible a huge housing boom. There was, however, a fatal flaw – once a mortgage had been securitised and sold, the original lender no longer needed to be concerned about the borrower's ability to meet the interest cost or eventually to repay the loan. This is what probably led mortgage companies to extend their lending to people in the United States who would never be able to pay – the so-called 'subprime' mortgages. In the UK too, banks – the extreme example being Northern Rock – and also some building societies began to lend recklessly, sometimes agreeing to a loan of a value even higher than that of the underlying asset, let alone what that asset – a house or a flat – might be worth in a falling market. Banks also began to accept self-certification of income from mortgage applicants. People with self-certified mortgages that had been inadequately checked or with loans with a value that was higher than that of the asset on which they were based, would be in serious trouble if they became unemployed or if interest rates rose.

The original lender became even more removed from worry about ability to pay interest or redeem their loans when these securities were further sliced, diced and repackaged to form 'collateralised debt obligations' (CDOs). CDOs could themselves be further subdivided and repackaged into what were called 'CDOs squared'. By the time all this repackaging and subdividing had taken place, the risk on such bonds was widely spread. This was hailed by many people as an advantage, since any risk was well diluted and spread. But the fact was that few people understood the nature of these securities and no one dealing in them was able to assess the degree of risk they contained. Indeed, Robert Peston, in the excellent book *How Do We Fix This Mess?*, says that to assess the risk involved in all the mortgages that were contained in a CDO squared would take a diligent person seven years of constant reading if one assumes that there were 150 mortgages in every CDO involving a prospectus of 200 pages and 300 pages in every prospectus for a CDO squared.[2] Even the ratings agencies – Moody's, Fitch and Standard & Poor's – could not do this. They seem to have been taken in by those who claimed that risk was negligible because it was so widely spread. Amazingly, they gave triple-A ratings, the highest available, to these securities.

The banks used these securitised assets to augment their deposits as a base for their lending and, because they were so highly rated, they did not have to be covered with a substantial amount of capital, when it came to satisfying the international requirements for capital adequacy set out in the Basel agreements at the Bank for International Settlements. This is what led to disaster. It never seems to have occurred to those responsible that, at some point, these assets might not be able to be sold or might be sold only at a heavily depreciated price. Once the markets realised that many of these securitised assets were toxic, their value plummeted and they became impossible to sell. While Bank of Scotland had seen attractions in the merger with Halifax, because it offered the prospect of increased lending using the large Halifax deposits as a base, the new management of the merged bank went much further. The emphasis was not on assessing risk but on selling more and more loans. It sold their mortgages as securitised assets and extended lending far beyond the deposit base. Lending was very profitable and so it was encouraged, not only to expand what was already the largest mortgage book of any of the UK lenders, but especially in the commercial loan sector where Peter Cummings was in charge. He was a Bank of Scotland rather than a Halifax man but, encouraged by senior management, he excelled in increasing commercial lending.[3] The inevitable result was that, when the wholesale market dried up, HBOS became spectacularly insolvent and had to be rescued in a rushed merger with Lloyds TSB in which the government took a 43 per cent shareholding. When, in 2009, it became apparent that the HBOS losses were much larger than previously thought, the government announced that it would increase its stake in Lloyds Banking Group to 65 per cent.

After the crash, Cummings was severely criticised by the Financial Services Authority (FSA), disqualified from working in banking and made to pay a fine of £500,000. He would argue that it was successive chief executives, James Crosby and Andy Hornby, both of whom were from Halifax, who pressed him to increase lending by so much. It may be a mistake to lay all the blame on Cummings because many would argue that he would not have been able to do what he did if the old Bank of Scotland management had been in control.

So what might the government of an independent Scotland have done about this? There are those who will argue that a Scottish government and Scottish regulator would never have allowed the Scottish banks to get into such an overextended state. Well, maybe. But the Scottish First Minister was encouraging Fred Goodwin, chief executive of Royal Bank, a bank in which he himself had once worked, right up to the last. And being independent and having their own regulator did not stop Ireland, Iceland or Spain from getting into a similar mess. So a Scottish regulator would have had to be endowed with better foresight than any of the counterparts in these other countries. The fact is that almost no one foresaw the crisis developing in the way that it did.

Assuming that the RBS takeover of NatWest and Bank of Scotland's merger with Halifax had taken place, the crisis would obviously have required intensive discussions between an independent Scottish government and the government of the remainder of the UK to agree a joint plan. The rescue of Fortis in the three Benelux countries is sometimes quoted as an example of the sort of rescue that would have had to take place. Fortis was a conglomerate

– its banking operations included both commercial and investment banking but it also had a substantial insurance business. It was split up after the catastrophic attempt to take over ABN AMRO. The Dutch government nationalised the banking and insurance subsidiaries in the Netherlands. The Dutch banking business was renamed ABN AMRO and the insurance business was split off as ASR Nederland. The Belgian government eventually sold much of the remainder of the banking business to the French bank BNP Paribas. The rest of the insurance business, which was substantial in Belgium, remained with Fortis but its name was changed to Ageas.

Discussions between the governments were far from easy, involving a good deal of argument to get a fair division of the assets, and this led to several attempts by shareholders to take legal action before the deal was finally settled. A Scottish government would have had to be involved in similar discussions with the government of the remainder of the UK and there would be room for much disagreement, especially over the division of assets abroad. Probably the Scottish parts of HBOS (the old Bank of Scotland) and Royal Bank would have had to be nationalised at considerable cost, leaving the government of the rest of the UK to deal, in whatever way it chose to, with the parts of the two banks in England and Wales. International subsidiaries would probably have been put up for sale.

Much would obviously have depended on whether an independent Scotland was still using sterling, as the SNP government have stated to be their policy, and, if so, whether the Bank of England remained lender of last resort and the UK Financial Services Authority or the Bank of England was still responsible for regulating banks in Scotland. Since all of this is unknown, it is not very helpful to speculate.

However there are some points that can be made. If there was a separate Scottish bank regulator – and that would seem to be a requirement for a member state of the EU – responsibility for the activities of the Scottish banks and indemnification of any losses made by depositors would be in accordance with whatever Scottish bank insurance scheme was operated and ultimately with the Scottish government. But, if the operations of Scottish banks in England and Wales were carried out through subsidiary companies rather than merely branches, these subsidiaries would have to be subject to the regulator for the rest of the UK. Compensation of depositors in these subsidiaries would then be the responsibility of the insurance scheme operated in the rest of the UK and would ultimately lie with the UK government.

This became an issue with the collapse of the Icelandic banks, Glitnir, Landsbanki and Kaupthing, which had expanded recklessly during the boom years to the point where their combined debt exceeded by six times the annual output of Iceland's economy.[4] The depositors' insurance scheme for Iceland's banks gave protection up to 20,000 euros but it was inadequately funded to meet the costs of compensation when the banks collapsed. Icelandic depositors were compensated but those with deposits in Icesave, an online branch of Landsbanki operating outside Iceland, were not. The British and Dutch governments decided to fully protect retail depositors with accounts in Icesave and then tried to reclaim from Iceland the cost that the Icelandic insurance scheme should have covered. This amounted to 3.9 billion euros which was close to 50 per cent of Iceland's reduced GDP. To impose such a burden on Icelandic taxpayers, especially when the Icelandic population was less than that of the city of Edinburgh, was clearly unaffordable. A deal was proposed which involved payment over 15 years at an interest rate of 5.5 per cent. This was rejected by Iceland's population in a referendum. One can imagine that there would be a similar reaction from the Scottish population if they had been asked to meet the costs of compensating English and Welsh deposit holders of Scottish banks operating in the rest of the UK after they had recklessly expanded.

Iceland has been accused, before the EFTA Surveillance Authority, of not meeting the requirements of a European Economic Area directive aimed at ensuring that bank deposits were properly covered by insurance; it has also been accused of discrimination because Icelandic depositors were compensated but those abroad were not. However another Icelandic bank, Kaupthing, owned the UK bank Singer and Friedlander as a subsidiary company. No claim could be made on Icelandic taxpayers for compensation in this case since it was regulated by the UK authorities and any compensation required would be a charge met by the UK insurance scheme.

What would have happened had Scotland been independent at the time of the banking crisis would therefore have depended on how the banks were organised and regulated at the time. Had NatWest and Halifax been set up as subsidiary companies for which the regulating authority was for the rest of the UK, there would have been a charge on the UK bank insurance scheme and no liability on the Scottish scheme or on Scottish taxpayers. But, had there been branches in England of the Scottish banks, the same liability would have arisen as affected Iceland. The Scottish insurance scheme would have had to pay and, if that was inadequate, there would have been recourse to the Scottish government and ultimately to Scottish taxpayers.

But compensating depositors of failed banks is not the only issue. As what has happened in Ireland demonstrates, the banks have other major obligations and costs. If a bank fails, the shareholders stand to lose their money, but what about those who hold bank debt in the form of bonds? In the global financial market, these bonds are held very widely across the world by other banks or by institutions such as pension funds. The Irish government guaranteed all these liabilities and it is said they were pressed to do so by the European Commission, because of the knock-on effects on banks and institutions such as pension funds all across Europe if they did not do so.[5] But it proved a major mistake. Bonds, after all, should not be regarded as risk free – that is why the interest on bank and company bonds is higher than on gilt-edged securities. To have simply allowed the banks to go bankrupt would have caused a lot of people to lose money but it would probably have been preferable for Ireland. The costs of meeting the banks' liabilities were much higher than the Irish government had estimated and overwhelmed Irish state finances. Although Ireland's government had been in a strong financial position with a surplus on its budget before the crisis and its debt in relation to GDP one of the lowest in Europe, the guarantee of the banks' liabilities imposed such a heavy burden that the government had to seek a bailout from the IMF, the European Central Bank and the European Union.

I believe that, had Scotland been an independent state in 2008, it would not have been able to cope with the losses incurred by its banks, whatever arrangements had been put in place, and, even if the banks and the Scottish authorities had had the foresight to ensure that operations outside Scotland were conducted by subsidiaries regulated in those countries, they would have had to face the same problems as Ireland. Indeed, none of the Irish banks were on the scale of Royal Bank or HBOS. If this had happened – and I think it would have – the Scottish government's finances would have been overwhelmed and, like Ireland, it would have had to seek a bailout from international organisations.

But what is past is past. So what are the lessons to be learnt for the future? Clearly other countries have to learn lessons too. One obvious lesson is that it is dangerous for banks to grow so large in a small country that they cannot be supported if they fail. Another is that normal retail banking should not be put at risk by investment activities that, however profitable, could jeopardise the viability of the bank.

The UK government set up the Vickers Commission to recommend action that needs to be taken. It has recommended increased levels of capital to support lending so that banks have a larger cushion against insolvency. This is clearly important and welcome. The commission also recommended ring-fencing the investment activities of banks to keep them separate from retail banking.[6] Others, including the Parliamentary Commission on Banking Standards, chaired by Andrew Tyrie, have questioned whether this goes far enough. It appears that they would like to see the ring-fence 'electrified' and the legislation contain a reserve power for complete separation. The intention is that investment or 'casino' banking should be sufficiently separate so that it could not put ordinary retail banking at risk and, if necessary, be allowed to fail in a crisis. A large combined bank cannot be allowed to fail because of the dire consequences for the whole economy. In that situation, investment bankers get huge bonuses if they do well but, if they do badly, there is an unwritten guarantee from government that they will not be allowed to fail. My own view coincides with that of the Parliamentary Commission – that the Vickers' recommendation, despite being unpopular with the banks, does not go far enough.

Scotland has a substantial financial sector, employing a

lot of people. Its banks were one of the features that made Scotland distinctive and they have been a source of much pride in the past. That is why the failure of the two large banks was so keenly felt. The first lesson must be that there are grave dangers in having banks that have so clearly outgrown the size of the economy, as was evident in Iceland. Many people take the view that Britain's banking sector, even against the size of the UK economy, is too large to the point at which it poses a risk. So, if Scotland becomes independent, it should aim at having a banking sector that would not overwhelm the economy if things go wrong.

There also needs to be much tighter control of credit. As Robert Peston shows, after the banks started using mortgage-backed securities to increase their lending, they reached a point where there was a shortage of borrowers – banks were more or less throwing loans at people, accepting self-certification for mortgages, as well as offering mortgages at very high loan-to-value ratios.[7] Credit was rising at a much faster rate than the growth of the economy whereas, before Big Bang, it had risen at approximately the same rate. So long as it lasted, lending was highly profitable. Now the situation is in reverse as the banks try to rebuild their balance sheets.

An aspect of this that has not yet been addressed but which, in my view, is very important is the connection between lending and housing policy. It is no accident that, in the UK, Ireland and Spain, all countries that got into serious difficulty, the proportion of home ownership in the housing stock was extremely high. It is now about 70 per cent in the UK and, although it used to be much lower in Scotland, the gap has almost disappeared with owner occupation about 66 per cent of the total stock. In Germany, on the other hand, less than half of the housing stock is in owner-occupation and it is even lower in Switzerland. In

France it is not much over 50 per cent. In Britain, since the 1980s, home ownership has been strongly encouraged by government and Right to Buy on heavily discounted terms has resulted in tenants buying much of the local authority stock. There has also been a remarkable housing boom, only made possible by the great expansion of bank lending. This long-lasting boom led to a tripling of house prices in the decade and a half up to the peak in 2007. People came to expect house prices always to rise and to rise faster than inflation or earnings. It had not always been so. At the end of the 1980s, there was a sharp drop in house prices for several years. But that was forgotten and people came to think that a house was an investment on which one could not lose and that it was worth taking out a huge mortgage to provide funds for other things, such as an expensive holiday or luxuries of various kinds, because, with house prices going up, there would be never be any difficulty in paying it off.

Obviously people aspire to own their homes. It is the preferred form of tenure for most people. But it is dangerous if people are encouraged to take on the burdens of ownership when they cannot really afford it or will be unable to afford it if interest rates rise, as inevitably they do from time to time. Despite interest rates being very low at present, the newspapers are reporting that a high proportion of owners are in difficulty with their mortgages. Some are paying interest only, having stopped the element of repayment. Others have difficulty even with the interest. The threat of possible repossession causes a lot of pain and anguish. Other countries have a much larger, properly regulated rented sector – some of it social rented from housing associations and some of it privately rented.[8] The former is at below commercial rents with an element of subsidy, the latter is market determined. In both cases, the landlord takes responsibility for maintenance, which can involve major unexpected costs that an owner-occupier in financial difficulty could find it hard to afford. For those on low incomes whether in work or unemployed, those who are disabled and have little or no income and people who fall on really hard times, Housing Benefit is available, along with other benefits.

It is a feature of any modern society that there is a section of the population that cannot afford homes of a standard that society considers acceptable. In the old days, that led to slums and, to get rid of slums, we built council housing. The quality of some council housing, although better, also left a lot to be desired. The experience of Europe, especially in Scandinavia but also now in Scotland, seems to show that social housing can be best provided through housing associations. But there also needs to be a strong private rented sector of good standard for people who may have to move often or who do not yet feel able financially to take on the responsibilities of ownership.

Much of the excessive lending by banks has been connected with housing debt. It is no kindness to encourage people who cannot afford it into home ownership. It causes hardship for the people concerned and ultimately, when there are defaults, serious damage to the lenders, with consequences for the whole economy.

So an independent Scotland would have to think hard about its banks: what size the financial sector should be; how it should be regulated; whether that requires a Scottish regulator and a Scottish lender of last resort; and how, if it has activities in other countries, they should be structured so as not to cause an insupportable burden, should they fail. I see no evidence that the Scottish government has done much of this thinking so far. But the connection with housing policy is important, because it has accounted for so much of the excessive lending. Any thinking on the future of banking in Scotland therefore needs to be coupled with a reappraisal of housing policy to consider how the population can have a good quality of housing without the pain of being stretched beyond what individuals can afford and of how this can be provided without the financial sector taking risks in lending that put the prosperity of the country at risk.

6

Scotland's Energy Future

Under the Scotland Act of 1998, which established devolution, energy policy is a reserved matter for the UK government but the Scottish government has responsibility for planning decisions. This means that it could refuse permission for new developments, such as a nuclear power station, and that planning decisions for developments such as wind farms, though initially for local government, rest ultimately with Scottish Ministers. They also have responsibility for an agreed proportion of electricity to be generated from renewable sources under the Renewables Obligation (Scotland). This division of responsibility may appear unsatisfactory and is probably not understood by many people but appears to have worked quite well. Certainly the Scottish government has developed its own view on energy policy and, as planning decisions are involved in most aspects of development, such as wind farms, it is right for them to do so.

In the summer of 2011, there was a debate in Edinburgh organised by *The Spectator*. The subject was 'Scotland's Energy Policy is just Hot Air'. There were speakers for and against this motion but a large majority at the end of the debate supported the motion. There were many who criticised the Scottish government's policy but little was said about the responsibility of UK Ministers. What was particularly evident in the debate was concern – and, indeed, hostility – about the effect of the widespread development of wind farms on Scotland's landscape. It also seemed that there was a good deal of scepticism about climate change.

My own view on climate change is quite simple. I am not a climate scientist but I respect the overwhelming view of those experts who study the subject. This is that climate change is real and that, although there have been major changes in climate over a long period, the only plausible factor that can account for the changes that have been observed over the last century or so is the increased release of greenhouse gases caused by human activity. Apart from changes in temperature, it is also predicted that there will be more extreme weather events and certainly experience of recent years seems to bear that out.

In a major report published in 2006, the Scottish Environment Protection Agency (SEPA) found that, since 1961, there had been significant changes in Scotland's weather – Scotland had become much wetter.[1] Although there have been large variations from year to year, there had been an increase in average winter precipitation of 60 per cent in the north and west and an average annual increase for the whole country of 20 per cent. Some parts of north-west Scotland had become up to 45 per cent drier in summer. The average period of snow cover had decreased over 40 years as a result of milder autumn and spring temperatures. The sea level around Scotland had risen and the seas had warmed by 1 degree Celsius over the last 20 years, causing changes in the abundance and distribution of marine species. A successor to this report has not been published but the findings of other studies confirm the changes that are taking place and SEPA has published its own Climate Change Plan.[2]

There are still quite a number of climate change deniers. But, whether one accepts the findings or not – and I do – the issue is of such importance and the consequences potentially so serious that it would be foolish to do nothing.

Lord Nicholas Stern in his important review for the government argued that, while policies to try to halt climate change were expensive, the consequences of doing nothing could be catastrophic for the world and would cost a great deal more.[3]

I therefore welcome the Scottish government's targets for replacing dependence on fossil fuels with renewable forms of energy. These targets have been revised and are ambitious. At a conference in Glasgow in October 2012, the First Minister said that it was now intended to have 50 per cent of Scotland's electricity demand supplied from renewables by 2015. He felt it was possible to achieve this because Scotland had met 35 per cent of demand from renewables in 2011, as against a target for that year of 31 per cent. The aim is now to meet the equivalent of 100 per cent of Scotland's electricity demand from renewable sources by 2020, and the Scottish parliament has passed legislation requiring greenhouse gas emissions to be cut by 42 per cent by the same date.

Scotland is well endowed with a wide variety of energy sources. Coal production provided the energy for the industrial revolution in the 18th and 19th centuries. At its peak, the output of coal was over 20 million tonnes a year but it is the most carbon-emitting form of energy and all of the deep mines in Scotland are now closed. However, a considerable amount of coal – some 6 million tonnes a year – is still produced from opencast workings and is used in Scottish power stations.[4] North Sea oil and gas are both now past their peak production and are expected to continue to decline but the output is still substantial, as we will see in Chapter 7. Imports to the UK from other sources are now growing and, in the case of gas, now account for about half of the supplies in the UK; but the output of both from the North Sea still greatly exceeds Scotland's requirements and will remain significant for at least another generation.

The Royal Society of Edinburgh in its major *Inquiry into Energy Issues for Scotland* found that 34 per cent of total energy was required for domestic use, some 28 per cent for transport, 21 per cent for industry and 16 per cent for services.[5]

Electricity Generation

About a quarter of energy used in Scotland is required to make electricity but, as Table 1 shows, a substantial 23 per cent is exported through the interconnector to England and a further 3.5 per cent to Northern Ireland. So Scotland is a major exporter of electricity with more than a quarter of its output going to other parts of the UK. In 2011, 33 per cent of Scotland's electricity was generated by nuclear power, 21 per cent by coal, 15.7 per cent by gas, 27 per cent by renewables (hydro 10.4 per cent and other renewables 16.4 per cent) and 2.3 per cent by oil.[6]

Most of the electricity produced is now generated in four large power stations with a combined capacity of 7,229 megawatts (MW): one coal-fired – Longannet; two nuclear – Hunterston B and Torness; and one gas-fired at Peterhead (see Table 2). Most of these are now quite old, the most recent being Torness, which was commissioned in 1988. Cockenzie, a coal-fired power station which had a capacity of 1,200 MW, no longer met EU emission standards and closed in March 2013, but it may get a new lease of life if Scottish Power's plans for a new gas-fired plant on the site are implemented. The largest plant, Longannet, is more than 30 years old but it has been upgraded with flue gas desulphurisation scrubbers to reduce emissions of SO_2 and NO_x, the gasses responsible for acid rain; it has also been adapted to enable gas to replace 20 per cent of the

Table 1

Scottish Electricity Generation and Use 2011

	GWH	percentage
Coal	10,779	21.0
Gas	8,052	15.7
Oil	1,156	2.3
Nuclear	16,892	33.0
Hydro	5,936	10.4
Wind, wave and solar	6,992	13.7
Other renewables	1,404	2.7
Waste	12	1.2
Gross Total Supply	51,223	100
Pumped storage and own use by major generators	-2,924	5.7
Own use by other generators	-353	0.6
Transmission and Distribution losses	-2,444	4.8
Net total supply	45,502	88.8
Exports to England	-11,597	22.6
Exports to Ireland	-1,769	3.5
Supplied to Scottish consumers	32,136	67.5

Source: Department of Energy and Climate Change, Energy Trends,
December 2012

coal and will burn environmental waste composed of heat-treated dried sewage sludge. Hunterston B has just had its life extended to 2023 while Torness can also be expected to have its life extended in due course. Peterhead, which was repowered with increased capacity in 2000, should have considerable life left too. So it is likely that, one way or another and in contrast to what was expected till recently, all five plants (if a rebuilt Cockenzie goes ahead) could remain operational for many years yet.

Table 2

Electricity Generating Capacity (Main Producers) 2011

	Capacity in MW
Coal	
Longannet	2,400
Cockenzie	1,200
Gas	
Peterhead	2,177
Nuclear	
Hunterston B	1,288
Torness	1,364
Hydro	
Natural flow	1,489
Pumped storage	720
Wind and Wave	3,016
Other renewables*	305
Total Renewables**	4,810

*landfill gas, sewage gas, other bioenergy
**excluding pumped storage
Note: Figures are for maximum capacity which will be greater than capacity available at any one time.

Source: Department of Energy and Climate Change, Energy Trends,
December 2012

In 2011, there was 5,685 MW of capacity in renewable power stations, an increase of 1,042 MW or 22 per cent on the previous year. But this capacity is not available all the time – it depends on the amount of water for hydro and wind for wind farms. The hydro stations, since they were first developed, have been a major economic benefit to Scotland. Unlike the renewables now being developed, they have not required subsidy. They are individually much smaller than the five large fossil-fired and nuclear stations, ranging from just a few megawatts to over 100 MW. Combined, they have a considerable capacity but many of them have insufficient water resource to run their turbines all the time and are designed to store up the water to use it to run their turbines to meet peak demand. For this, they are extremely valuable, particularly in complementing the nuclear stations, which are base-load stations that cannot readily be turned off and on. The fossil-fired stations are more flexible than nuclear, especially Peterhead which burns gas, but they still take a considerable time to start up or to close down. Demand for electricity is highly variable, depending on time of day, time of year and temperatures. Moreover, a key feature of electricity is that it cannot easily be stored, so that there has to be capacity to meet the highest expected peak demand. The flexibility of the hydro stations is therefore of great benefit to the whole system.

To the natural flow hydro stations, most of which date from the 1940s and 1950s, has recently been added the large Glendoe plant with a capacity of 100 MW. In addition to these are the two pumped storage schemes at Cruachan and Foyers with a combined output of 700 MW and an ability to store the equivalent of 1,510 MW in the form of their water resource. These do not add to the total supply but use off-peak electricity to replenish their reservoirs so that they are available to generate at full power during peak periods. Scottish and Southern Energy have recently announced plans for three more pumped storage schemes, including two large ones in the Great Glen at Loch Lochy and Invermoriston. Together, these will add a further 900 MW of capacity. They also intend to convert the existing Loch Sloy scheme at Loch Lomond to provide a further 60 MW of pumped storage capacity.

No power station has a 100 per cent load factor. There have been major and sometimes prolonged outages at the nuclear plants and even the fossil-fired stations have to have their boilers shut down for maintenance. But, in the renewable sector, the load factor is much lower. The Scottish hydro stations have a load factor of about 45 per cent simply because there is not sufficient water in the reservoirs to run the turbines all the time. But this is manageable. Installed capacity is deliberately more than can be run full time. Its output can therefore be planned and, although rainfall varies, there is enough in Scotland, especially in winter, to generate as much power as is required.

Wind power is much less predictable. The load factor for onshore wind in Scotland in 2011 was 27.4 per cent, only marginally better than in England. For offshore wind, it was higher, 35.8 per cent but, as yet, there are relatively few offshore wind farms. Very often, when the weather is coldest in winter, an anticyclone over the country means there is very little wind. This, coupled with the major impact that wind farms have on the landscape and the subsidy that is still required, has led a lot of people to question the value of investment in wind energy. It means too that other forms of energy have to be available as backup; that requires investment in plant which may be only intermittently required.

The subsidy for wind power is provided through Renewables Obligation Certificates (ROCs) and the Climate Change Levy. These require the power companies to meet targets for the generation of renewable energy but, inevitably, that puts up the cost of the electricity supply that has to be met by consumers. Since Scotland has much more wind power than either England or Wales, it follows that consumers in England and Wales are meeting part of the subsidy for wind energy in Scotland. This is an important issue for the independence debate. A Scottish government might find that English and Welsh consumers were unwilling to subsidise Scottish wind power electricity if Scotland was a separate country. This, however, might depend on whether the rest of the UK was able to meet its renewable energy targets by some other means or, despite the requirements of clean energy, decided to ignore them.

The response to this is usually that England and Wales will still want electricity exports from Scotland. But, if their own supplies of electricity cannot cover their needs, they would seek the cheapest supplies available. This might still be electricity from Scotland but, if they thought that too expensive, they would have the options of additional investment in England and Wales or of importing supplies through the interconnectors with the Continent.

However, by the time Scotland becomes independent, if it does, onshore wind power could be virtually economic without subsidy. Bloomberg New Energy Finance has forecast that onshore wind power will be economic by the second half of this decade, as a result of economies of scale and improvements in technology. This accords also with the view given by various experts in evidence to the House of Commons Select Committee on Energy and Climate Change.[7] But much will depend on how prices move for other forms of energy, an issue which I touch on later. Offshore wind generally causes people (with the exception of Donald Trump) less environmental concern over its visual impact and has a better load factor but is, at present, much more costly. Here too costs are likely to come down in time as technology develops but for, the foreseeable future, investment in offshore wind is unlikely without significant subsidy.

In the meantime, there are further substantial developments planned for wind farms. If the aim were to replace the two nuclear stations with wind farms as they come to the end of their lives, a great deal of additional capacity would be required. Although the present wind and wave capacity (3,016 MW) is theoretically greater than that of the two nuclear stations (2,653 MW), with a load factor of only 27 per cent, it would be far from enough. Just to match the annual output of the nuclear stations, something like a tripling or quadrupling of wind capacity would be needed. It is claimed that Scotland has potential for 11,500 MW of onshore wind farm capacity and even more, about double this amount, offshore where the load factor is better but the cost is higher. But these figures for potential capacity take no account of the intermittent nature of the supply. Obviously a lot of Scotland would be covered with wind farms and the present hostility to them would, understandably, become very much more intense. There is also concern about their effect on tourism because of their impact on the landscape. These worries may well be justified but they could become much more serious if there is a huge amount of additional development. There would then be strong pressure on politicians and local planning authorities to oppose it.

In my view, it is essential, if wind farm development is to be acceptable, for local communities to get benefit from it. Here the small development of three turbines by the island community of Gigha is an interesting example of how this can be done. The development by Viking Energy, a joint venture of Scottish and Southern Energy and the Shetland

Charitable Trust, is another. This is a large development and it now has planning permission, although opponents against it are still active; it will consist of 103 turbines with a capacity of 370 MW. The advantage is that Shetland has far more wind than mainland Scotland, as demonstrated by the existing small Burradale wind farm, which has a load factor averaging 52 per cent. The output of Viking Energy would be far in excess of Shetland's needs and the intention is to export it by cable to the mainland. Such a cable, however, would itself be an ambitious project, which still has to be financed and built. Nevertheless, it is estimated that the Shetland Charitable Trust could get an income from its investment in Viking Energy of over £20 million a year, dwarfing even the substantial income the islands get from North Sea oil.

There are ways in which the variability of supply can be mitigated. The hydro stations can complement wind power, as already mentioned, and the additional pump storage schemes to be built by Scottish and Southern Energy will add considerably to this flexibility, making power available when required and when the output from wind is low. There is scope for some further hydroelectric development and pump storage capacity if needed.[8] The development of other forms of renewable energy may also help to mitigate the peaks and troughs of wind energy.

A great deal of work is being done on the development of wave and tidal energy – especially in Orkney, where the tidal flow in the Pentland Firth is exceptionally strong. Tidal energy in particular, although intermittent, is much more predictable than wind energy. But, although these developments offer promising prospects and the resource is reckoned to be considerable, the technology is in its infancy and it will be many years yet before it is able to be developed on a commercial basis. The pioneering PURE project in Shetland, which uses two small wind turbines to make hydrogen, could also be a way of storing energy when it is not required and to make it available when it is. Manufacturing hydrogen from wind power is also of interest in providing energy in more remote areas, where costs of linking to the grid are high; Western Isles Council aims to follow the example of Iceland in using hydrogen to power its public transport.

But perhaps the best way to tackle the intermittency of wind power is by extending the grid, on the principle that the wind will always be blowing somewhere – in Shetland, Orkney or the Western Isles, if not on the Scottish mainland. It is with this in mind that the First Minister has had discussions in Norway about an undersea cable linking the two countries. The problem with this would probably be the cost but it is worth investigating further. Already, in addition to the grid interconnectors linking Scotland to England and Ireland, England is linked to the European continent from which it is a net importer.

The Viking Energy project in Shetland will test the viability and cost of a long undersea cable. The company's assessment indicates that the cost of the cable would not destroy the viability of their project. There has also been a recent report of a proposal to run a cable from Iceland to the Scottish mainland to deliver geothermal electricity, which is abundant and cheap, from Iceland's volcanoes.[9] Apparently this was considered some years ago and rejected on cost grounds. It would require a cable of 1,000 kilometres, the longest sea cable in the world, and go through much deeper water than the cable from Shetland but Landsvirkjun, the Icelandic electricity producer, believes that it may now be viable. If it went ahead, it could provide a valuable means of balancing any irregularity in production from Scotland's renewable energy.

These proposals highlight the importance of access to the grid at reasonable cost. There has been much complaint about this, with renewable power sources in the north and west of Scotland being expected to pay much more for a connection than power sources nearer the market in the south of England. This is, of course, an economic matter – absence of long distribution lines involves less cost to the grid and means that power sources nearest to the market would expect to pay less than those furthest away, especially if there is a shortage of power in the south and a surplus in the north. But the cost of connection to the grid could make some of the best renewable sources of power uneconomic to develop. This therefore needs to be subjected to rigorous scrutiny to ensure that these costs are reasonable and can be justified.

The report of the Royal Society of Edinburgh's Inquiry argued for a mixture of electricity suppliers so as not to be too reliant on one source, bearing in mind the uncertainties that there are. A proposal from Scottish Power for an experimental carbon capture plant at the Longannet coal-fired station was rejected by the UK government on grounds of cost. But a proposed carbon capture and storage (CCS) plant by Shell and Scottish and Southern Energy linked to the Peterhead gas-fired power station together with a proposal from a consortium at Grangemouth are on the short-list and await an early decision. These would inject carbon into oil fields in the North Sea. If the technology succeeds, it would provide a way of making emission-free energy from fossil fuels, which could be very important for the future. But, even if it is successful, the costs for the foreseeable future are likely to be high.

So the future for energy supplies in Scotland has plenty of promise. Scotland undoubtedly has exceptional renewable resources and the technology will continue to develop.

There would seem to be two main dangers. The first is a public backlash if the view strengthens that ever-increasing wind farm development is damaging the landscape; but it is fair to say that it is much easier to decommission a wind farm after 25 years than to decommission a coal-fired station let alone a nuclear plant. The second is that the wider market for Scotland's renewable power resources may not materialise as hoped, for instance because grid connections prove too expensive to finance or heavy investment in English shale gas removes the pressing need for additional electricity from renewable sources.

The 'Fracking' Question

Already the hydraulic fracturing revolution, known as 'fracking', has resulted in a huge drop in gas prices in the United States, where they are now less than half the price for gas in Europe. It apparently holds out the prospect of the United States becoming once again self-sufficient in gas and oil. Indeed, the International Energy Agency has forecast that the United States will overtake Saudi Arabia in oil production by 2020, as a result of oil from fracking.[10] If so, this will affect the international oil price, but gas markets are much more local, as gas is less easily traded. If similar developments take place in Europe, however, it could affect gas prices in Britain, making the generation of electricity by gas powered plants, already probably the cheapest form of electricity generation, very attractive. This would be a cleaner form of energy than coal, but it would still release about half the amount of carbon of a coal-fired plant. If it were developed in place of clean energy, therefore, it would not enable Britain to meet its carbon reduction targets. But it could, through bringing down energy prices, make it more difficult to produce electricity economically from Scotland's renewable sources. This could obstruct investment in new renewable capacity, although projects already built would presumably continue to generate electricity since the marginal cost of wind power is close to zero.

At present, the scale of potential gas supplies from fracking in Britain, or indeed in Europe, is largely speculative. The exploration company Cuadrilla Resources has drilled three wells in Lancashire and is now drilling a fourth. But it has not, so far, been allowed to fracture and cannot flow test the wells to discover how productive the source is. In evidence to the House of Commons Select Committee on Energy and Climate Change, however, the company has said that it estimates the resource of the Bowland Basin at 200 trillion cubic feet of gas (tcf).[11] Not all of that will be recoverable but, even if only a small fraction is recovered, it will still be substantial, given that, in the peak year of 1999, output of gas from the North Sea was 4 tcf.

At present, the uncertainties surrounding shale gas are probably similar to those affecting North Sea oil when it was first discovered and it would be wrong therefore to put much weight on any of the estimates. But the resources in Lancashire seem promising as they come from shale more than a mile thick, which Cuadrilla Resources say is probably unique and is thicker than the shale being exploited in the United States. There is also a prospect of gas from fracking shale in Scotland and from parts of the North Sea where there is shale that was discovered in drilling for oil. Existing installations for oil in the sea could reduce the infrastructure cost of exploiting these reserves but at present that is highly speculative.

The importance of all this for energy policy in an independent Scotland is simply to emphasise the uncertainties. The huge drop in gas prices in the United States, as a result of the fracking revolution, is making industries that had become uncompetitive in international markets competitive again. Might it do the same in Europe? At this stage, one cannot tell but informed opinion seems to think it unlikely for a variety of reasons: there is likely to be much stronger resistance to development in densely populated parts of Europe, such as Lancashire, than in the sparsely populated areas of the United States, where much of the development is taking place; and, under European law, minerals underground are the property of the state, whereas in the United States they are the property of the landowner, who stands to benefit directly. This acts as a driver for development. In the UK, the most that seems to be suggested at present is that shale gas might be enough to stop dependence on imported gas from increasing further.

For Scotland, this means that, if the UK is to meet its climate change targets, the Scottish renewable energy resources will still be needed, unless alternative green energy can be found. As argued above, the subsidy on wind power is decreasing and the need for it may be eliminated for onshore wind by the end of the decade. But subsidy is likely still to be necessary for offshore wind and will certainly be needed for wave and tidal power, which are still only in the very early stages of development. If Scotland becomes independent, would consumers in the rest of the UK be willing to continue to pay the necessary subsidy for Scottish green energy? Might they find alternative green energy sources or would their lobbying make UK politicians abandon their carbon targets and simply go for fracking to get cheap gas?

North Sea Oil – the Mishandling of an Opportunity

Because economic issues have featured so prominently in the case for independence as set out by the SNP, the revenues from North Sea oil and gas have become a major part of the debate. As was shown in Chapter 1, Scotland, like the UK as a whole, has had a substantial budget deficit since the banking crisis of 2008 and the ensuing recession. Although the First Minister and others have argued that Scotland's deficit in the last few years has been proportionately less than that of the UK,[1] this has certainly not always been the case and it depends on the assumption that some 90 per cent or so of the oil and gas revenues would accrue to Scotland as an independent country.[2] This is based on the median line as estimated by Alex Kemp and Linda Stephen of Aberdeen University, both highly respected researchers on oil and gas. But, as I pointed out in Chapter 1, there are a fair number of assumptions involved in the First Minister's calculation, which cannot be taken for granted.

The reason this is so important is, as I also explained in Chapter 1, that Scotland has, and has had for many years, a higher level of public expenditure per head than the UK average. An assumed geographical share of the oil and gas revenues in the last few years would approximately compensate for this, though not to the extent of eliminating all of the present deficit. So the issue is whether these revenues can be relied on to continue at this level, or at least until, by some means, the economy can be made more productive, so that non-oil tax revenues are increased.

In 1974, when I was Chief Economic Adviser at the Scottish Office, I wrote a paper for Ministers which was obtained a few years ago under freedom of information. This paper, which sparked some controversy, was written as confidential briefing for Ministers at the time of the 1974 election. I argued that the then outgoing government in their public statements had underestimated the scale of the developments in the North Sea and that the revenues were likely, by 1980, to be very large. I went on to argue that the scale of these tax revenues made it no longer tenable to say that an independent Scotland could not manage financially. Scotland's economy, at that time, was in a worse condition than it is now, with many of its industries in difficulty. The paper was intended as something of a wake-up call for both Ministers and their officials, some of whom had not realised the importance of what was happening in the North Sea, and urged that stronger action, through regional policy and by other means, was needed to help the Scottish economy. Everything I said in the paper turned out to be right about the scale of the development and of the revenues. But the paper has become rather notorious and it has been claimed it was suppressed. That was not the case. Confidential briefing for Ministers is never published and, had I published it on my own initiative, I would have been breaking every rule and would have been in serious trouble. I did not think that what I was saying was so earth shattering. The paper was based on information mostly from public sources and at least one newspaper was making the same arguments.[3]

Graph 1
UK Crude Oil Production

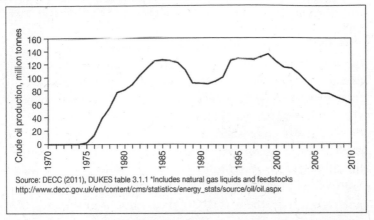

Source: DECC (2011), DUKES table 3.1.1 *Includes natural gas liquids and feedstocks
http://www.decc.gov.uk/en/content/cms/statistics/energy_stats/source/oil/oil.aspx

Graph 2
UK Gas Production

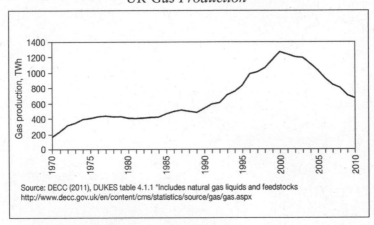

Source: DECC (2011), DUKES table 4.1.1 *Includes natural gas liquids and feedstocks
http://www.decc.gov.uk/en/content/cms/statistics/source/gas/gas.aspx

But that was 1974, and the situation was different then. Gas was already flowing to England from the southern basin of the North Sea and the network was being extended to Scotland. But oil production from the northern North Sea did not start until 1975 and only became substantial after 1980 (see Graphs 1 and 2). The big hikes in international oil prices, first in the mid 1970s and again in 1979, meant that, when oil production grew in the 1980s, the revenues generated for government were very large indeed, especially in the early part of the decade before the sharp fall in international oil prices after 1984. Oil prices have risen again from their low point in the 1990s and, in recent years, have been very high (Graph 3). Gas prices are much less volatile – although gas is being increasingly traded internationally, the greater difficulty in transporting gas means that, whereas the oil market is international, the gas price depends much more on local markets.

Graph 3
Crude Oil Prices

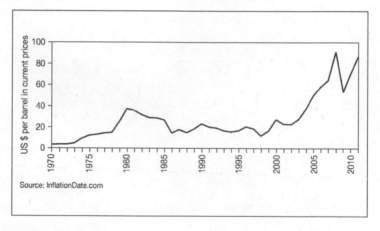

Source: InflationDate.com

Production and Outlook for Offshore Oil and Gas

What matters now is the present position and how it is likely to develop. Graphs 1 and 2 show that North Sea oil production peaked at 137 million tonnes in 1999 and offshore gas production at 1,260 terawatt hours (TWh) in 2000. By 2011, crude oil production was down to 52 million tonnes and offshore gas to 326 TWh – both less than half peak output. From 1981 to 2004, exports of crude oil from the UK had exceeded imports but, by 2011, exports were only equal to slightly over half the amount imported. That does not mean that offshore oil and gas are unimportant – their life has been extended beyond the original estimates, as more has been discovered, and it is now likely to last for at least another 30 or 40 years. How much will be produced and how long it will last depends on what new discoveries are made and on improvements in technology that enable a higher proportion of the oil and gas to be extracted from existing wells. Oil & Gas UK announced in April 2013 that production is expected to increase to some 2 billion barrels of oil equivalent* in 2017 compared with 1.5 billion in 2013. This follows a big increase in investment by the oil companies, notably by BP in its Clair Ridge project, a major field that should be in production till 2050. Nevertheless, over the long term, the decline in output of both oil and gas is expected to continue at a gradual rate, despite these developments. Alex Kemp, the official historian of North Sea oil and gas,[4] said at a recent hearing of the House of Commons Select Committee on Energy and Climate Change that this decline might be at a slower rate than in the last few years and oil output might stabilise for a period but he did not expect the decline to be reversed.[5]

The tax revenues, however, depend not just on the volume of oil and gas produced but also on international oil prices and on the profitability of the companies producing the oil. Tax revenue is obtained from both oil and gas but is much greater from the production of oil because price

---

* A term used in the industry, 'oil equivalent' means oil plus natural gas liquids all converted to the equivalent in oil.

depends on international rather than local markets. The most obvious feature of oil prices, however, is their volatility. After the high levels of the 1970s and early 1980s, the oil price fell sharply and remained low in the early 1990s. Today, the price is high again, although not as high as a few years ago. Gas production rose steadily to its peak in 2000 and oil production fell after 1985 but rose again thereafter to its peak output in 1999. The consequence of these price movements coupled with the trends in output was that tax revenues which had been very high in the early 1980s, reaching £12 billion in 1984/85, fell to around £1 billion in the early 1990s before rising again to a peak of £12.9 billion in 2008–09 (Graph 4). This latter peak, though high, is not actually nearly as high in real terms (allowing for inflation) as it was in 1984/85. If the revenues are recalculated using constant 2008/09 prices, they would have been £28 billion in 1984/85 (Graph 5).

Graph 4
North Sea Tax Revenue at Current Prices

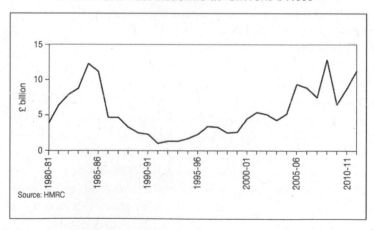

Source: HMRC

What is likely to be the level of tax revenue in future?
The independent Office for Budget Responsibility (OBR)
has estimated a sharp fall from £11.3 billion for the UK in
2011–12 to £7.4 billion in 2012–13 and to £4.5 billion in

Graph 5
North Sea Tax Revenue at Constant Prices

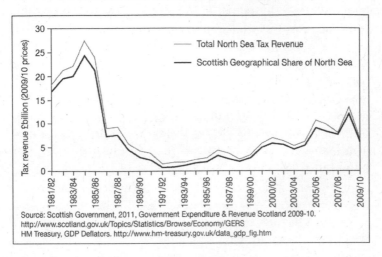

Source: Scottish Government, 2011, Government Expenditure & Revenue Scotland 2009-10.
http://www.scotland.gov.uk/Topics/Statistics/Browse/Economy/GERS
HM Treasury, GDP Deflators. http://www.hm-treasury.gov.uk/data_gdp_fig.htm

2017–18. This is based on forecasts of output, prices and
profits, all of which are inherently extremely hard to predict. It is probably as good a forecast as one can get but
inevitably it is subject to a wide margin of error. Many people expect oil and gas prices to remain high or even go up
higher. This may well turn out to be what happens if China
and India continue to develop at the speed of recent years.
Because both are such huge countries, demand from them
is likely to have a major impact on the market, pushing up
prices of many raw materials, including oil. Uncertainty in
the Middle East, the world's largest exporting region, is also
something that cannot be discounted. On the other hand,

the fracking revolution referred to in the last chapter has already greatly reduced gas prices in the United States and will affect the oil price too, especially if, as predicted, it makes the United States virtually self-sufficient in gas and oil. We have yet to see what impact fracking may have on European markets. So all we can really say is that future prices are uncertain. My own view is that they are more likely to go up than down over the longer term but the only thing one can be sure about is that they will be volatile and any forecast is likely to be wide of the mark.

The revenues from oil and gas also depend on the cost of producing it. As the most productive sources are depleted, it is to be expected that costs will go up. More marginal resources will be brought into production. Indeed, the large Clair field, west of Shetland, which is in water depths of over 500 feet and is now being developed, was earlier thought to be uneconomic. And, if advances in technology enable a higher yield to be obtained from existing wells, that too is likely to be at a cost. So, even if the oil price remains high or goes up further, it does not follow that profits and hence tax revenues would remain as high.

At the House of Commons hearing already referred to, Fergus Ewing, the Minister in the Scottish government responsible for energy, was asked about decommissioning costs when the rigs and platforms in the North Sea have to be removed. Professor Kemp had already said that these costs would have to be met by the oil companies when decommissioning started and that they would be a charge against their profits, thereby resulting in lower tax revenue. Mr Ewing, on the other hand, seemed to be arguing that, if Scotland became independent, the rest of the UK should meet part of the decommissioning costs because, for part of their lives, many of these fields had been generating profits for the UK. This would presumably mean that the Scottish government would expect the government of the remainder of the UK to pay some compensation for the reduced tax revenues accruing to the Scottish government after decommissioning starts. This strikes me as a very hard one to sell and one that would be bound to be resisted – especially as both the First Minister and Mr Ewing repeatedly assert that Scotland, with its share of the North Sea, would be the sixth wealthiest country in the world[6] (although, as we have seen in Chapter 1, this is based on GDP per head, which is not a good measure of wealth as it includes oil company profits received by shareholders, many of whom are not resident in Scotland).

The Case for an Oil Fund

The First Minister has argued for the setting up of an oil fund on the Norwegian model and has suggested that, if £1 billion was paid into this fund each year, it could be worth £30 billion in 20 years time. This would, of course, depend on whether it was possible to set aside £1 billion a year, when it would start and what rate of return could be expected. Ministers have tried to clarify the aim, saying that payments would be made into the oil fund as soon as fiscal conditions allow. This is a laudable aim – one that I strongly favour and argued for in the 1970s. In a paper that I wrote then, I made two main points: first that there was a danger of a sharp rise in the UK exchange rate in the 1980s, as oil production got under way and replaced imports, which could damage the rest of the economy; and second that part of the tax revenue should be paid into a special fund.[7]

As Alex Kemp explains in his *Official History of North Sea Oil and Gas*, this was considered seriously in the 1970s.[8] What Ministers in the then Labour government had in mind, however, was not so much a fund that would accumulate, as the Norwegian fund has done, but a fund to finance capital expenditure, such as key infrastructure projects or the modernisation of industry.[9] This was to include an emphasis on regional development in Scotland, Wales, Northern Ireland and the Development Areas of England. In the end, however, a majority of the Cabinet were against it. It should be remembered that, when this was considered, it was February 1978. The state of the UK economy was extremely difficult, with high inflation and balance of payments difficulties, and North Sea revenues had not yet begun to flow in any substantial quantity.

Although Alex Kemp reports that there was further discussion in the Treasury in the 1980s, the issue does not appear to have been considered by the Conservative government collectively. Instead, the effect of the oil and gas production on the balance of payments, coupled with the very tight monetary policy being pursued at the time, was to push the exchange rate up dramatically. The pound, having been trading at $1.60 in the late 1970s, rose to $2.40 in the early 1980s, with catastrophic consequences for much of manufacturing industry. In effect, the tax revenue from the North Sea ended up paying for the resulting unemployment.

The decade of the 1980s was the time when an oil fund should have been set up. If payments had been made into it then, continued in subsequent years and allowed to accumulate like the Norwegian fund,* it would, by now, have been worth a huge amount of money. The Norwegian fund was established in 1990 and receives the state's total cash flow from petroleum activities. It is the largest wealth fund in Europe, worth now some £330 billion, dwarfing the country's

---

* This is known as the 'government pension fund – global' – *Statens pensjons-fond – Utland* or SPU.

national debt and amounting to 70 per cent more than the whole output of the Norwegian economy in one year. The fund is required to invest this money abroad rather than in Norway, to counteract the effect it would otherwise have on the balance of payments and exchange rate. Much of the income from these investments also accrues to the fund and is reinvested, which accounts for its remarkable growth.

The UK has, of course, a much larger economy but a fund of this kind would have ensured that there would have been no doubt about the UK's credit in the present economic crisis and would have saved us much of the misery from the austerity we have been suffering. That such a fund was not set up, when it could have been, was very short-sighted and, in my view, a tragedy. It amounts to a serious mishandling of the greatest economic opportunity the UK has had in the last two decades of the 20th century.

If it becomes independent, would Scotland be right, even now, to try to set up an oil fund? What I take to be the aim of SNP Ministers is something more along the lines of the Norwegian fund than the sort of fund the British government was considering in the 1970s. Professor Kemp, in his House of Commons committee evidence, said, yes, it would be right, because using the oil revenues to pay for current spending is running down a capital asset, albeit a naturally endowed one, to pay for what should be funded by ordinary tax revenues. The Nobel Prize-winning economist Professor Joe Stiglitz has said the same.[10] The asset will disappear with nothing to replace it. I agree. It is just that it would be very difficult to do, when Scotland has as big a deficit as it has at the moment. If Scotland became independent and the oil revenues were immediately diverted to a special fund, the rest of the budget would be heavily in deficit. That would mean that there would have to be big tax increases or public expenditure cuts on top of what the coalition government has already imposed. The Scottish economy would be pushed into an even worse recession and the level of unemployment would rise even further. I do not think that is practical. So I agree with the Scottish government's declared policy of putting the oil revenues into a special fund as soon as fiscal conditions allow. That should not be taken as a licence to put it off indefinitely, but as the economy's growth looks likely to be feeble for some years, it may be a considerable time before reducing the deficit would enable significant amounts to be set aside.

The Shetland and Orkney Oil Funds

The only parts of the UK with the foresight to set up oil funds from which they could benefit were the Northern Isles. Shetland pioneered this arrangement. Under the leadership of its then Chief Executive, Ian Clark, the council set up a fund into which oil companies were required to make a 'disturbance' payment for oil passing through the terminal at Sullom Voe. It required the oil companies to share a properly planned common user terminal, which some of them had been reluctant to do, and because so much – probably nearly half – of the oil was in waters for which Shetland was the nearest landfall, the amount of oil going through the Sullom Voe terminal was very large indeed. The proceeds, based on the throughput of oil, have been paid into the Shetland Charitable Trust, which now has assets in excess of £210 million and income able to finance expenditure of approximately £11 million a year. Orkney Islands Council followed the example of Shetland with a smaller fund based on the oil flowing through its terminal on the island of Flotta.

Shetland has used its money for a variety of charitable purposes of benefit to the local community. There are first-class leisure centres in all the main population settlements, there is exceptionally good care for the elderly, including specially built homes and visiting day carers, which reduce the burden that would otherwise fall on the NHS. There is investment in property to let and in a district heating scheme, both of which yield a return. The Trust has also part-funded the excellent Shetland Museum in Lerwick. But perhaps most significant of all will be the investment, along with Scottish and Southern Energy, in Viking Energy's proposals for the large wind farm referred to in the last chapter. If this goes ahead, it could give further major financial benefit to the islands.

With so much of the oil in Shetland waters, Tavish Scott, the MSP for Shetland, has pointed out that his constituency is in a very strong position in the Scottish independence debate. Together with Liam McArthur, the MSP for Orkney, he has submitted a paper to the UK government emphasising the distinctive position of the Northern Isles. The islands were incorporated into Scotland by an Act of the Scottish parliament in 1472 but they have their own separate identity, of which they are very aware, stemming from their Norse heritage.

There are some in London who have suggested that, if Scotland becomes independent, Shetland might prefer to stay as part of the United Kingdom. I have never thought this likely but, as Tavish Scott says, the Shetlanders are in a strong bargaining position if they care to use it. The centralising tendencies of Scottish governments since devolution are not welcomed in the islands and Shetland is conscious of the advantages its neighbours, the Faroe Islands, have as a dependency of Denmark rather than an integral part of the Danish state. In this respect, they are analogous to the Isle of Man or the Channel islands, which are British dependencies. The Faroe Islands are not part of the European Union, although they have unrestricted trade access to it. This has enabled them to retain control of their own fishing policy, an industry on which the islands heavily depend, and which is also of great importance to Shetland.

Brian Wilson, the former MP and Energy Minister, writing in *The Scotsman*, is clearly aware of some of the feelings in Shetland and, with his long association with the Western Isles, has suggested that all three island groups have something to gain from a change to their status.[11] At the time of writing, it would not surprise me if we hear a good deal more of this. As Scotland moves towards the referendum, it would seem right, both for those in favour of independence and for those against, to give some thought to this issue, if indeed there proves to be a demand for change. With so much of the oil in the waters off these islands and their great potential also for renewable energy, it would be a huge mistake not to take the matter seriously, whether Scotland becomes independent or not.

Conclusion

The main point that has emerged from the discussion in this chapter is the great uncertainty surrounding so many of the issues relating to North Sea oil and gas. We know now that the resource is likely to last much longer than was originally thought and to remain important for many years yet. But we also know that output is past its peak and declining gradually. The price of oil in future international markets is very uncertain. There was an expectation that it might continue to rise as a result mainly of rising demand, especially from the Far East and other developing countries, and that may still prove to be right but the fracking revolution could make that less certain. All that we can be really sure about is that the future is impossible to predict but that prices are likely to be very volatile, just as they have been in the past. This volatility will affect the taxation revenue that an independent Scotland could expect to receive. Will a rising oil price compensate for a reducing output? This uncertainty could make it very difficult for those who would have to manage the government's budget. The proposal to set up an oil fund is to be commended but it would be very difficult at present to put any revenue aside without either raising taxes or cutting public expenditure further than it is being cut already. It is only realistic to expect that there will be a lot of pressure to use the money for other pressing needs. As far as the Northern Isles – the only part of Britain that has been wise enough to set up such a fund – are concerned, it would be a great mistake to ignore any aspirations they may have to resist the tendency to increased centralisation or for some change to their status. The islands are of critical importance to Scotland, whether it becomes independent or remains part of the UK, both for their key position in relation to offshore oil and also their huge potential for renewable energy.

Welfare and Inequality

Government expenditure on social protection is the largest single programme in Scottish public expenditure, as it is also in the UK. In Scotland it cost over £21 billion in 2011/12, 38.4 per cent of all identifiable public expenditure, compared with almost £19 billion for health and education combined (see Table 1).* It includes the State Pension and benefit expenditure for the disabled, the unemployed and those with low incomes, as well as Housing Benefit and care for the elderly. Over 70 per cent of this expenditure, some £14 billion is the responsibility of the UK Department for Work and Pensions (DWP) and therefore not devolved; and rates of State Pension and benefits are therefore the same throughout the UK. Of the remainder, less than £1 billion is paid directly by the Scottish government and some £5 billion by Scottish local authorities.

Given its huge cost, it is obviously important to consider where the main responsibility for welfare should lie – whether with the UK Parliament, as it is now, or with the Scottish government and Parliament. Although the Scottish government's role in social protection is at present limited, much of the expenditure for which Scottish Ministers are responsible is closely related. Health, for example, is a Scottish government responsibility, as are education and

---

* Identifiable expenditure excludes defence, foreign embassies, interest on the National Debt and other items that are costs for the UK as a whole and cannot be allocated to a particular part of the UK.

skill training and housing. The Scottish government pays for Free Personal Care but Attendance Allowance is paid by the DWP. Scottish Ministers in the present government have said they would like complete responsibility for welfare, which they would have, of course, with independence or Devo-Max but not with most of the other proposals put forward for devolution. And the findings from the 2012 Scottish Social Attitudes Survey showed that nearly two thirds (64 per cent) of Scots think that benefit levels should be the responsibility of the Scottish Parliament.[1]

Table 1
Scottish Identifiable Public Expenditure 2011–12 *

	£ million	percentage
General Public Services	1,093	2.0
Public order and safety	2,416	4.4
Economic Affairs**	4,961	8.9
Environmental Protection	1,056	1.9
Housing and Community	1,719	3.1
Health	10,989	19.8
Recreation, culture and religion	1,224	2.2
Education and training	7,702	13.9
Social Protection	21,323	38.4
Accounting adjustments	2,999	5.4
Total	55,481	100

*excludes international services, defence and debt interest
**including enterprise and economic development, agriculture, forestry, fishing, employment policies, science and technology and transport

Source: Government Expenditure and Revenue Scotland 2011–2012, *March 2013*

Expenditure per head in Scotland is above the UK average by some 7 per cent and is expected, for demographic reasons, to grow more rapidly, as Professor David Bell has shown in a paper for the David Hume Institute.[2] This is mainly because the proportion of the Scottish population over age 65 is higher than in the UK as a whole and is increasing faster but also because there is a higher proportion drawing benefits for illness or disability, which tend to increase with age. Thanks to advances in medical care, many more people in all developed countries, including Scotland, are living longer and this involves increasing cost. But the ratio of working population to dependents is the key issue. Although recent figures show that the years of net emigration from Scotland seem to be behind us and the population is growing, it is doing so more slowly than in the UK. This is partly because there has been less immigration to Scotland than to other parts of the UK and also because immigrants tend to have larger families.

In view of its scale, how money is spent on welfare matters a great deal and there is an obvious need to make it as cost-effective as possible, especially at a time when public expenditure throughout the UK is being cut. This applies to Scotland at least as much as to the UK. Several interesting points emerge from the breakdown of the expenditure in Tables 2.1 and 2.2, some of which may be surprising to those who have regarded welfare benefits as something that could and should be cut – the State Pension accounts for 45 per cent of the total DWP expenditure and, if other items that are age-related are added, such as Pension Credit, Attendance Allowance and Disability Living Allowance (DLA) for pensioners, it is more than half. DLA itself, including not only pensioners but children and those of working age, accounts for almost 10 per cent, and Incapacity Benefit together with Income Support for those drawing

Table 2.1

Expenditure by UK Department for Work and Pensions on Benefits in Scotland 2011–12*

	£million	percentage
Attendance Allowance	481	3.4
Bereavement Benefit/Widow's Benefit	59	0.4
Carer's Allowance	153	1.1
Council Tax Benefit	384	2.8
Disability Living Allowance	1,372	9.8
of which children	109	
of which working age	774	
of which pensioners	488	
Employment and Support Allowance	381	2.7
Housing Benefit	1,728	12.3
Incapacity Benefit	564	4.0
Income Support	670	4.8
of which on Incapacity Benefit	418	
of which lone parents	190	
of which carers	34	
of which others	28	
Industrial Injuries Benefits	93	0.7
Jobseeker's Allowance	461	3.2
Maternity Allowance	24	0.2
Over 75 TV licences	49	0.4
Pension Credit	752	5.3
Severe Disablement Allowance	97	0.7
of which working age	75	
of which pensioners	21	
Statutory Maternity Pay	197	1.4
Winter Fuel Payment	188	1.3
State Pension	6,325	45.2
Total	13,978	100

*excludes tax credits

Source: Department for Work and Pensions, Expenditure tables, as revised
April 2013

this benefit a further 7 per cent. Housing Benefit accounts for 12 per cent. These are the largest items. The cost of unemployment, if Jobseeker's Allowance and Employment and Support Allowance are taken together, is only around 6 per cent. Among the items for which the Scottish government is responsible (see Table 2.2), the cost of free prescriptions is very small, when compared with these other items, and the cost of concessionary travel is not very large either but the cost of Free Personal Care and Free Nursing Care is significant and is expected to increase considerably as the population ages.

Table 2.2
Scottish Government Expenditure 2011–2012

	£million
Concessionary travel	249
Free prescriptions	57
Free Personal Care	427
Free Nursing Care	23

Source: David Bell's paper 'Social Protection in Scotland' given to the David Hume Institute

The UK Government's Reforms

The UK government's reforms to welfare are driven not just by the need to control expenditure; there are also serious faults in the present system. There are a bewildering number of different benefits, as more have been added to over the years. This can be confusing to claimants and involves having to fill in numerous claim forms, which some deserving people, especially those with serious disabilities, find difficult. According to the DWP, this can result in some people getting less benefit than they are entitled to and gives scope for fraud. But that is not the only problem – those taking low-paid jobs can lose as almost as much in benefit, when they start employment, as they gain from earnings. This poverty trap has been a problem for many years; it can discourage those on benefit from taking jobs, if the pay they will receive is not significantly more than the benefit they will lose. Everyone has heard anecdotal evidence, whether reliable or not, suggesting that there are some people on benefit who could and should be working. This may well be so, especially if the only job available to an unemployed person involves work which they regard as unpleasant and with a pay that makes them little, if any, better off. I have never been able to understand why some politicians have so strongly argued the case for incentives for the better off, such as businessmen and bankers, while at the same time ignoring the need for incentives for poorer people.

For all these reasons, the need for reform was widely accepted. Given the scale of the task, however, with so many existing types of benefit and tax credits, it is a formidable undertaking and tackling it is bound to throw up unexpected problems. Nevertheless this is what Mr Duncan Smith's Universal Credit is intended to achieve. Reform would be needed just as much in an independent Scotland. But for such a reform to be acceptable, the gain must be clearly seen to outweigh the loss from the inevitable upheaval; and the present time is, in many respects, the worst time to be attempting it. It would be much easier when the economy is buoyant than at a time when few jobs are available and the Treasury is determined to achieve savings, even if it causes much resulting hardship.

According to the government's updated Impact Assessment of December 2012, the replacement of the many existing benefits by Universal Credit, which will be phased in from the autumn of 2013 until completion in 2017, should actually increase payments to households by £0.3 billion.[3] Most of those gaining, it is claimed, will be among the poorest groups in society. But some 2.8 million households will receive less benefit. So, even if there are more gainers than losers and the gainers are those most in need, the effect on many people will be very painful. On top of this, the Welfare Benefits Up-rating Act of 2013, which will limit the rise in benefits, most tax credits and Universal Credit to only 1 per cent a year, while inflation is running well above 2 per cent, will result in a much larger number falling into poverty. According to a report for the Scottish Council of Voluntary Organisations, hardship will be increased for many people of working age who are already struggling.[4] In addition to this, there will be a benefit cap of £500 a week for a couple or lone parent and £350 a week for single people. This will apply to all benefits except Disability Living Allowance, War Pensions or Working Tax Credit. There is a real danger that what is an ambitious and necessary reform will be seen just as a savage attempt to save money. Although Universal Credit only starts to be implemented in the current year, the indications are not good.

Disability Living Allowance (DLA), which will not be part of Universal Credit, is not means-tested but many people have simply had their benefit stopped and been made to reapply, no matter how serious or permanent their disability. This is causing great distress, even if benefit is eventually restored, as was shown when a blind man with heart trouble and diabetes, whose benefit had been stopped, gave evidence to the Scottish Parliament. Both the newspapers and television have carried similar stories of cases where the stopping and then reassessment for DLA has caused immense distress. In some of the cases one hears about, the person is so obviously unable to work that one wonders why the benefit was ever stopped. DLA is to be replaced by a Personal Independence Payment (PIP) which, like DLA, is not to be means-tested but the budget for it is being cut by 20 per cent and all claimants will have to go through a reassessment process, which will be repeated at intervals. This process itself involves considerable cost to the taxpayer and one may question if it is necessary where a person has a permanent disability.

More than 60 per cent of those on Incapacity Benefit, which was subsumed into Employment Support Allowance (ESA) in 2008, have also had their payments stopped. Although quite a high proportion of them also get their benefit restored on appeal, as Martin Sime, chief executive of the Scottish Council for Voluntary Organisations, has said, the effect on many poorer people is likely to push them to despair.

There is also concern about the proposal for cutting Housing Benefit if the claimant is assessed as not needing as much accommodation as their current dwelling provides – the so-called 'bedroom tax'. It is understandable that the state should not pay for more accommodation than is needed. But, unless the assessment is done with care, it can give distressing results. Cases have arisen where a person is told that they have one more bedroom than needed, although a carer uses that bedroom on frequent needed visits. And it makes no sense to cut someone's benefit and tell them they have to move to smaller accommodation if such accommodation is not available in the neighbourhood where carers and others who look after them live.

Inevitably, the cost to the country of welfare benefits goes up when the economy goes into recession. People lose their jobs and swell the ranks of the unemployed, just as tax revenue falls. Many of those who do manage to get work find that they have to take part-time work or jobs that are less well paid than they had before. Even if not unemployed, they may be drawing benefit in the form of Income Support. There seems to be a widely held view that public expenditure on welfare is excessive and it is certainly large but, according to David Bell's analysis, if expenditure on health is included, the UK comes approximately in the middle of the range for European countries – not only the Scandinavian countries but France, Germany, Italy, the Netherlands and Belgium all spend more on social protection as a share of their GDP.[5] The best way of reducing the country's bill for benefits would be to get out of recession and back to full employment, though that would do little to reduce the cost of welfare benefits for older people, which account for around half of the total cost.

One of the welcome features of the reform, however, is to reduce the poverty trap by revising the tapering of benefits when a person taking a job starts to earn an income. The present taper can result in a person losing the equivalent of more than 90 per cent of their income. In future, this 90 per cent taper will be reduced to 65 per cent. This is certainly an improvement but it still means that a person taking a poorly paid job could lose more than half of their income. Reducing the taper is very expensive, as it involves paying out benefit when previously it would have stopped and it must be one of the reasons the cost of the welfare policy remains so high. But, unfortunately, at a time when the economy is in recession and job opportunities are extremely scarce, it is fanciful to suppose that this will enable many of those who are unemployed to get a job, even if they try their best to find one.

Poverty

The Chancellor unwisely castigated many of those drawing benefit as shirkers and contrasted them with the strivers who found a job and went out to work. The truth is, however, that there are 6.1 million in work drawing benefit because, with low incomes, they are still in poverty and they outnumber the 5.1 million who are not working at all.

Since the late 1990s, according to research done for the Joseph Rowntree Foundation, there has been a welcome reduction in the numbers classified as living in poverty.[6] This was the result of the high level of employment before the financial crisis and of measures, such as tax credits and increases in benefit, introduced by the last government. The Institute for Fiscal Studies calculated that, for lone parents in work, there was an increase in income of 12 per cent, while the proportion of households receiving out-of-work benefits fell by a third.[7] It had been the government's stated aim to end child poverty by 2020. Obviously the recession put an end to that but the prospect now is for the numbers in poverty, both adults and children, to increase.

Over the last thirty years, inequality in our society has greatly increased, as it has also in the United States and many other countries.[8] The better-off, especially but not only in the financial sector, have been able to increase their incomes enormously, while those on the lowest earnings have gained much less and, in some cases, hardly at all. This is a consequence of globalisation, technical change and, in the financial sector, of deregulation. As poorer countries have developed, especially in the Far East, cheap goods have come to Western markets that have kept prices down and forced many manufacturing firms in Europe and North America either to give up production or to reduce costs by restraining the growth of wages so that they can compete. This phenomenon is also described as the 'disappearing middle' – the loss of skilled manual and lower management jobs through computerisation, more advanced capital equipment and competition from abroad.

This runs counter to the kind of Scotland that many people would like to see. With the dominance of SNP and Labour, it is often claimed that Scotland is a more social democratic country than England, where the Conservative Party is still strong. Some commentators writing in the Scottish press have argued for much greater equality of income, as is typical of Scandinavia, or at least for a more caring society with much greater attention paid to the deprived areas in the cities and to those whose prospects of employment and a decent income are poor.[9] This is a type of society that I strongly favour myself but we do not know what the Scottish electorate as a whole would vote for. Doing more for the less well-off would involve a greater tax burden for the better-off, and the recent Scottish Social Attitudes Survey, despite finding that a majority favoured greater devolution of welfare benefits, did not suggest that there was an appetite among the general public for this type of redistribution. But Scandinavian levels of welfare support would inevitably require Scandinavian levels of taxation. It would also require us to be as competitive as the Scandinavians are in global markets.

Where Should Responsibility for Welfare Policy Lie?

All of this means that where the responsibility for welfare lies is a major issue in the constitutional debate and likely to become an increased focus of attention. Not only is it a very important area of policy and a major part of public expenditure but it might also be expected that the different balance of politics in Scotland should be reflected in policy choices. It is necessary, therefore, to consider what scope for policy choice could be available to a Scottish government both with independence and greater devolution.

With independence, the Scottish government would have

complete control of welfare policy, along with all its other responsibilities. But even that does not mean it could act without considering what was happening in the rest of the UK. Scotland is so integrated with the other parts of the UK economy that movement of population across the border would always be very easy. This would mean that, if Scotland was more heavily taxed to an extent that was significant, there would be some businesses and people who might move to England; the opposite tendency would be apparent if Scottish taxes were lower than in the remainder of UK. Differences in welfare provision, if substantial, might also encourage benefit migration. Some people have apparently told those carrying out surveys that they would vote for independence if it made them £500 better off. One should take all this with a pinch of salt. There are some differences in tax rates and welfare provision between Swiss cantons that apparently do not have a huge effect. But the degree of Scotland's integration with the rest of the UK, which would remain even with independence, would certainly have some restraining effect on the scope for independence in policy.

Under various forms of devolution, the issue becomes more complicated. Those who would like to see the whole of welfare expenditure devolved need to consider whether it would acceptable, not only in Scotland but in the other parts of the UK, for different systems to be applied on each side of the border, while still remaining within one state. Would it be acceptable in Scotland and the rest of the UK if the State Pension and the various benefits for people who are unemployed or have low incomes were at different rates? The response to surveys does not favour that and there would be many who would be strongly against it. Since these are financed at least in part by national insurance, which is at the same rate in Scotland as elsewhere in the UK, people would argue that benefits should also be the same.

Although the main responsibility for welfare rests with the UK government at present, the Scottish government is not powerless in this area. Free prescriptions and care for the elderly provide significant welfare benefits. So too does the provision of social housing, action to improve Scotland's areas of acute deprivation and the provision of skill training to help people into jobs. The UK government's welfare reform will result in responsibility for Council Tax Benefit being devolved. The European Agricultural Policy also provides social benefits, albeit in a way that is not effectively targeted at the poorer members of the farming community.

There are other parts of the welfare programme that would seem capable of being devolved: Housing Benefit is to be part of Universal Credit but would seem an obvious candidate, as the Scottish government is responsible for social housing; other possibilities are Maternity Allowance, TV licences for those over 75 and Industrial Injuries Benefits, but these are all small. Attendance Allowance, Widow's Benefit and Carer's Allowance might make sense in view of the Scottish government's existing responsibilities in health. Perhaps Personal Independence Payment (replacing the Disability Living Allowance) and Severe Disablement Allowance should also be considered, although differences here between England and Scotland might be more difficult for some people to accept and, if extreme, could encourage benefit migration. These items, apart from Widow's Benefit, are all non-contributory and not means-tested. They cost £3.5 billion in 2011–12 or 25 per cent of the present expenditure by the Department for Work and Pensions and, if devolved, would be in addition to the relatively small amount – less than £1 billion – for which the Scottish government already has direct responsibility and the £5 billion paid by Scottish local authorities. But, if these benefits were devolved, it should be remembered that, for demographic reasons, their cost is likely to escalate faster than for the UK as a whole.

Already there is a growing amount of disquiet in England about free prescriptions in Scotland, free care for the elderly and no university tuition fees for Scottish domiciled students. This is linked to the belief that Scotland gets too generous a share of funding through its block grant. How the grant is settled and whether or not it is too generous has already been discussed in Chapter 1. Differences in welfare provision that were thought to be to the advantage of the Scots would certainly aggravate this concern. If, on the other hand, the English got something that was not available in Scotland, the Scottish population would not be slow to complain.

This leads straight back to how the Scottish government is funded. The only way in which substantial differences in the benefit system between Scotland and the rest of the UK could be acceptable on both sides of the border would be if they were funded by devolved financial arrangements that people on both sides accepted as fair. It is normal in federal or quasi-federal countries for the central government to at least part-fund the budgets of the component states or regions, even if they have substantial tax powers of their own, but the arrangements need to be acceptable to all parties.[10]

In Scotland's case, the more that can be financed by taxes raised in Scotland, the more readily will differences in provision be accepted. The increased taxation powers available under the Scotland Act 2012 will go some way towards this and, if those taxation powers were increased further, as suggested in Chapter 2, that would again increase flexibility. But, for the remainder, a smaller block grant from central government would have to be based on a widely accepted system of needs assessment. If Scottish people then wanted a more generous provision of welfare, they would either have to pay more tax, perhaps with a higher rate of income tax that was directly hypothecated to the higher level of benefits, or accept that other programmes would need to be cut to provide the resources.

Even with the changes proposed above, the responsibility for at least the greater part of welfare expenditure including the largest item, the State Pension, would remain with the central government. This may seem unsatisfactory to many people who would want to see their government set quite different priorities from those applied by UK governments. But, under any feasible devolution scheme, however much it is adjusted to give more responsibility to Scotland, it seems inevitable that the main direction of policy on welfare has to rest with the UK. Even with independence, although in theory a Scottish government could set its priorities any way it wished, the real world would impose constraints. There would still be a need to curb public expenditure to balance the budget. And the close economic integration of Scotland with the rest of the UK, which is bound to continue even if it became less in time, would mean that significant differences in tax levels, in State Pensions and in welfare could become an issue and result in people moving to where they thought they could get the best treatment.

9

Conclusion

Those supporting Scottish independence sometimes point out that few, if any, of the countries that have seceded from a larger state regret that decision. Certainly the Irish Republic would not want to come back into the United Kingdom, nor Iceland to Denmark or Norway to Sweden; nor probably would the countries that have left the Soviet Union want to go into union again with Russia. But, in the case of Scotland, there has been no history of exploitation or bad government, such as fuelled the drive for independence in Ireland. Scotland is a relatively well-off country and could perfectly well be independent if that is what the people choose. Its economy is certainly much stronger than Ireland's was in 1922. But that does not mean that the process of separation would be easy or painless. It would be a major upheaval with uncertain consequences. It has been the purpose of this book to try to clarify the economic options and consequences of both independence and a greater degree of devolution so that people can understand what would be involved before voting in the 2014 referendum.

Scotland is among the wealthier countries in Europe with a GDP per head (excluding the North Sea) approximately equal to that of the UK and an unemployment rate very similar. Immigration has replaced net emigration and, on most measures, Scotland's economy is in a better relative position compared with the UK as a whole than thirty years ago. After more than 300 years of union, however, our economy has become very integrated with the rest of the UK. This applies especially to the capital and labour markets. We share many of the same institutions. Many Scottish families have a member or relative resident or working elsewhere in the UK. Like the rest of the UK, however, Scotland has been badly hit by the present recession. This is because, like several other countries in Europe, notably Ireland and Spain, the previous boom was fuelled throughout the UK by ever-expanding private debt, much of it associated with housing. When this came spectacularly to an end, the consequences and necessary adjustment were, and still are, extremely difficult and painful.

If the Scottish people decide in the 2014 referendum that they want their country to become an independent state again, the difficult circumstances of the recession, with unsustainable budget deficits and high public debt, which, at the time of writing, is still rising, do not make it the best time to choose. The first major problem would be with the Scottish government's own finances. The SNP government argues that Scotland's deficit is smaller proportionately than that of the UK. But that depends on some key assumptions that are set out in Chapter 1: the first, that Scotland would get, as its geographical share, some 90 per cent of the North Sea oil revenues; and the second, that the UK national debt would be divided on a population basis, rather than its share of UK GDP, including GDP from the North Sea. These are both subject to negotiation, the outcome of which must remain uncertain until negotiations for independence actually take place. There is, at present, no formal division of the North Sea between England and Scotland and negotiations between the UK and other countries over their share of the continental shelf have not always been straightforward. Sometimes they are protracted and may lead to arbitration. Even if, under international rules,

Scotland does get the bulk of the oil and gas revenues as expected, a decision on that could affect the share of the national debt Scotland was expected to take. And, after all that is settled, it would be up to the markets to decide what rate of interest had to be paid on Scotland's share of the national debt and on any new borrowing. Since those who own UK debt would probably not be happy with a share of it simply being transferred, the mechanism would probably involve the Scottish government having to float its own debt for the amount to be transferred and then paying the proceeds to the UK government so that the appropriate share of the UK debt can be redeemed.

For many years, Scotland has had a level of public expenditure per head which has been 10 per cent or more above that of the UK. With taxation revenue per head, excluding the North Sea, about equal to that of the UK, this leaves a gap that revenue from the North Sea would be needed to fill, unless expenditure was cut sharply. Even with this, there is, at present, an unsustainable deficit, as there is also for the UK, which is why the government's programme of austerity has been necessary (although whether the UK government has got the exact balance right between austerity and growth is a matter for debate). Unfortunately, the output of both oil and gas from the North Sea is now well past its peak, although its life has been prolonged as a result of new discoveries and advances in technology. The output of both is therefore expected to continue to decline gradually. In a few years, according to a Cabinet paper leaked to *The Scotsman*, which uses estimates from the Office for Budget Responsibility, this could result in revenue from the North Sea falling sharply and Scotland's future deficit becoming proportionately worse than that of the UK.[1] This, however, depends not only on the output but also on the price of oil and that is extremely difficult to predict. The oil price may rise further and more discoveries may be made, offsetting some of the impact on revenue of the predicted fall in output, but this is not something to be relied on. The potential impact of 'fracking', the process of hydraulic fracturing for oil and gas that has had a big impact on energy prices in America, also makes forecasting future prices exceptionally difficult. Because of both price and output variations, an additional problem is that the revenues have been very volatile, even in the last three years during which they have varied between £12.9 billion in 2008–09, down to £6.5 billion in 2009–10 and up again to £11.3 billion in 2011–12. This could make a future Scottish budget difficult to manage.

Alex Salmond has said that, as soon as circumstances allow, an independent Scottish government would put part of the oil revenues into a special fund, as Norway has done. I welcome that. It was a great economic opportunity missed that successive UK governments have not done this over the last 30 years. It would have transformed the UK's financial position. But, in the immediate future, Scotland would be unable to afford it. If Scotland becomes independent and if oil revenues are to be put into a special fund, its public expenditure will have to be paid for from non-oil tax revenue, which would be insufficient to cover it. Despite many assertions that Scottish control of economic levers would result in higher economic growth to pay for this, no one has really explained how that is to be achieved. Without it, cuts in expenditure would be necessary. A large proportion of the North Sea hydrocarbon resources are in waters off the Northern Isles. Shetland and Orkney both had the foresight to set up oil funds from which they have got considerable benefit. They are concerned now about a tendency towards centralisation of Holyrood governments and issues have been raised by their MSPs about their constitutional status within Scotland. The Scottish government would be well advised to discuss this with them.

If, on the other hand, Scotland remains in the UK, the British government is no more likely to put oil revenues into a special fund than its predecessors. I expect total Scottish public expenditure would eventually have to be brought to a level justified by a proper needs assessment so that it can be defended against criticism from other parts of the UK. But, if, as many experts expect, that did require a significant adjustment, it should be planned over a long period.

If Scotland becomes independent, the choice of currency is of crucial importance.[2] Whereas the Scottish government was previously in favour of joining the euro, it now wishes to retain sterling. There would need to be negotiations with the rest of the UK to determine on what basis that would be acceptable. If agreement was reached, all decisions on monetary policy would remain with the Bank of England. Scotland might hope to have some influence on such decisions but, whether there was formal involvement or not, the Bank of England would be bound to set its policy primarily to meet the needs of the remainder of the UK since it would comprise over 90 per cent of the combined economy. Furthermore, the problems in the eurozone have illustrated the difficulty of running a monetary union without close coordination of fiscal policies. It is therefore to be expected that the price Scotland would have to pay for a sterling monetary union would be control by the rest of the UK over its fiscal policy. This would involve not only the size of any budget deficit Scotland might have but probably also the need for some tax rates to be agreed – corporation tax would be the most likely – to avoid unfair competition. Whether the monetary union would last, however, would, in the end, depend on the view taken by the markets, as the break-up of the Czech and Slovak monetary union after less than six weeks (referred to in Chapter 3) clearly illustrated.

After independence, I would expect Scotland and the rest of the UK to diverge gradually in the policies they followed. Whether the SNP or Labour was dominant in Scotland, the balance in Scottish politics would be likely to be Social Democratic, whereas the UK, especially without Scottish members in Parliament, would be more likely to be Conservative. Scotland may wish to become a bit more like Scandinavia, with its comprehensive welfare system and relatively egalitarian society, whereas the rest of the UK, and England especially, might put more emphasis on a low tax, low public expenditure and free market economy, like the United States. If that happens, it could put severe strain on a monetary union. For these reasons, while I think it would be sensible for an independent Scotland to remain with sterling at least initially, it might prove difficult in the long run; and, to gain freedom to follow its own policies, it might be necessary for Scotland to have its own currency. This could be pegged either to sterling or the euro but, in a serious crisis, to avoid the kinds of stresses that we have seen in the eurozone, the exchange rate could be adjusted. Any risk of exchange rate adjustment, however, would, of course, be reflected in the interest rates the market would demand on Scottish government bonds.

Because the financial sector is so important to Scotland, the government after independence would have to think carefully about how it should be handled. The collapse of Scotland's two largest banks was a disaster keenly felt by many Scots, who regarded them as part of what made Scotland distinctive. To many, they had been a source of some pride. If Scotland had been independent at the time, I believe that their problems would probably have overwhelmed the country's finances, just as the insolvency of the Irish banks did in Ireland. It is important to learn from that experience so that, if Scotland does become independent, policies are in place to ensure that it could not happen. That means not only tight regulation and not having institutions that are too big to fail but also ensuring that Scottish-based banks and other financial institutions trading outside Scotland do so through subsidiaries, rather than branches, so that they are subject to the regulations and the deposit insurance scheme of the country where they operate. Keeping sterling as the currency would probably help Scottish financial companies because, if there was to be a separate currency, some of those whose main client base was not in Scotland, such as Standard Life, might wonder if they would be better to base their activities south of the border. There is, however, no reason why a small country cannot have a flourishing financial sector – Switzerland and Luxembourg are examples – but only the companies can say what they would do and their needs must taken into account in government policy.

It is clear that there would need to be negotiations for Scotland to become a full member of the European Union in its own right. The key to a successful outcome would be the goodwill of all the 27 member states and any others, such as Croatia, that might join before negotiations started. If there was such goodwill, it might be possible, as Sir David Edward has argued, for this to be done by Treaty amendment rather than by the full process of an Accession Treaty. It might also be reasonable to expect the other member states to agree conditions that would include opt-outs from the Schengen Agreement and the euro. But any one state could exercise a veto and the risk is that a country such as Spain, worried about secession movements in its own territory, might do so to avoid a precedent being set. I see no prospect of Scotland being able to retain a share of the UK rebate. Circumstances have changed since the UK rebate was originally negotiated and most countries would like to see it ended. Scotland would get substantial payments both from the Common Agricultural Policy and the Structural Funds and, although it would be making a net contribution to the EU budget, it would probably be no higher per head than that of several other countries.

The Scottish referendum will take place before the UK referendum on continued membership of the EU that the prime minister has promised if his party gains an outright majority after the next election. This commitment appears to be partly a consequence of a growing English nationalism, the most obvious manifestation of which is the rise in support for the United Kingdom Independence Party (UKIP); but there is also irritation with the rules and directives, many of which are associated with the single market. Encouraged by a strongly euro-sceptic press, opinion, especially in the south of England and in parts of the Conservative Party, is now actively hostile to the EU. That creates a difficulty for Scotland. If Scotland becomes independent and negotiates to stay in the EU but the rest of the UK then votes to leave, that could mean border posts at Gretna, Carter Bar and Berwick. The present expectation of those who wish to leave the EU, however, is that they could maintain a free-trading relationship and be within the single market, perhaps as a member of the European Economic Area (EEA). That may not be as straightforward as they assume. The other possibility is that, if Scotland votes to stay in the UK but then in the UK referendum also votes for continued EU membership while England votes to leave, it could create a difficult political situation and be a source of tension between the two governments.

Membership of the EU is very important for Scotland because so many inward investing companies have chosen it as a base from which to serve the European market. If Scotland was outside the EU, it would be more difficult to

attract inward investment and, depending on what agreement was reached on access to the single market, some of
those already in Scotland might leave. Trade negotiations
with countries outside the EU are conducted by the European Commission on behalf of all the member states. This
is a major benefit. In a world that is becoming increasingly dominated by large powers such as Brazil, Russia, India and China (known as 'the BRIC countries'), as well as
the United States, small European countries acting on their
own would have very little clout in such negotiations. So the
need for inward investment, unrestricted access to the EU
single market and influence in trade negotiations all make
membership of the EU of great importance to Scotland. If,
therefore, it seems increasingly likely that the UK will leave
the EU, the logical consequence could be an increase in support for independence.

Even excluding North Sea oil, Scotland has energy
resources that many other European countries would envy.
Output of renewable energy is increasing and will supply
a growing proportion of our electricity. But the visual
impact of more and more wind turbines on the landscape
is encountering ever-stronger opposition. Apart from this,
although land-based wind-power may be economic by the
second half of this decade according to forecasts, that is far
from the case with offshore wind power or with wave or
tidal power. More than a quarter of the electricity generated
in Scotland is exported via interconnectors to England and
Northern Ireland; and the subsidy for renewable energy,
regardless of where it comes from, is paid by consumers
throughout Britain. That is a cost which Scottish consumers
alone would find excessive and an independent Scotland
probably could not afford. Whether the rest of the UK would
be prepared to continue paying for it would depend on how
seriously the UK government regarded its commitments to

reduce carbon emissions and on whether it was possible to get cheaper supplies from elsewhere. This might be either via more investment in other parts of the UK or through the interconnectors with continental Europe.

Welfare is the biggest item of public expenditure in Scotland and responsibility for the bulk of it is not devolved. Out of a total expenditure of £21.3 billion, the Scottish government is responsible at present for rather less than £1 billion and Scottish local authorities about £5 billion, leaving the remainder, including expenditure by the Department for Work and Pensions and tax credits, as the responsibility of the UK government. If Scotland became independent, it would simply take all of this over and the amount it decided to spend would depend on its priorities and what it could afford. The various proposals for devolution, however, would leave the main responsibility for welfare with the UK.

The reform that is currently taking place to the UK welfare system was badly needed because of its bewildering complexity and in order to reduce the poverty trap. However, it has come at a time when the government is trying desperately to cut what it spends because of its budget deficit, and its effects are already causing much anguish, especially from the poor and disabled. This looks likely to become a major issue for the government, provoking not only criticism but outright hostility and unpopularity. It could become one of the most important issues by the time of the referendum.

Scotland at present gets 7 per cent more than its population share of the UK's welfare expenditure. Since the same system is operating throughout the country, this difference is mainly explained by Scotland's demography – in particular the larger proportion of elderly people. The latter factor results in higher expenditure on the State Pension and it is also the main cause of higher payments of Disability

Living Allowance. The proportion of elderly people in the population is rising in all advanced countries, causing expenditure on State Pensions and on various welfare benefits to rise; but the expectation is that this will be more marked in Scotland than in the UK as a whole. This is because the proportion of dependent population is rising more rapidly north of the Border and total population growth is slower there than in the parts of the UK where there has been a large flow of immigrants. None of the proposals for further devolution, other than Devo-Max, advocate devolving responsibility for the State Pension or benefits for those out of work. The reason is a view that different rates on these programmes would be unacceptable. However, I argued in Chapter 8 that responsibility for some benefits, amounting to about 25 per cent (£3.5 billion) of expenditure by the UK Department for Work and Pensions, might be considered for transfer to the Scottish government, although it should be borne in mind that, because of Scotland's demography, this latter could be a burden that rises more rapidly than for the UK as a whole. Furthermore, if such a transfer is not to play into the hands of people in other parts of the UK who already think Scotland's block grant is too generous, it would need to be accompanied by increased responsibility for taxation.

In Chapter 2, I argued that three quarters, though not all, of income tax might be devolved in addition to the smaller taxes in the 2012 Act and also some of those referred to by the Campbell Committee, as explained in Chapter 2. I also suggested that most of the proceeds of VAT could be assigned but not devolved (a possibility mentioned in the Calman report); this is because EU rules do not allow different rates within one member state.[3] Many people regard assignment of revenues, where rates cannot be altered, as pointless. But it would make it clear to those elsewhere in the UK that a much higher proportion of public expenditure – over half, including the additional expenditure on welfare – was paid for by taxes raised in Scotland. Such an arrangement would leave Scotland more exposed to fluctuations in revenue caused by changing economic conditions and it might therefore be necessary to increase the Scottish government's power to borrow. But it would also give the Scottish government the benefit of the growth of its economy and encourage the adoption of policies to achieve that. The block grant would be much smaller but, to avoid it still becoming an issue of contention, there would need to be a plan to move it gradually, when circumstances made it possible, on to a system based on an agreed assessment of needs.

So there is a lot to think about if Scotland becomes independent – many of the unknowns would depend on the outcome of negotiation. Some of these – the choice of currency in particular – are of enormous importance. Much could go wrong and it is impossible at this stage to know whether the added flexibility in policy that independence would bring would make Scotland stronger in the long run, or whether people would be worse off. Inevitably it would be a bumpy ride at first and, for many people, disillusioning till things got a chance to settle down and those responsible for government had learnt what they could and could not do. After Ireland became independent in 1922, it was a long time – at least a generation – before policies were adopted that began to bring the country to the high level of prosperity it was able to achieve and, despite the severe effects of the financial crisis, still has. I would not expect that to happen in Scotland but it would take some time. There has been a tendency in some quarters to think that North Sea oil revenues will pay for everything. That is clearly not so.

At the time of writing, a majority vote for independence in the 2014 referendum looks unlikely. But a lot can happen in 18 months and the UK coalition government, as it struggles with reining in its budget deficit, may become increasingly unpopular. If independence is rejected, however, there is a real danger that politicians at Westminster and officials in Whitehall may think that they can put away the files and not worry about Scotland any more. Proposals for increased devolution might then be shelved. That is quite a likely outcome but it would be a huge mistake. It would probably mean that the next time there was a big surge in support for independence in Scotland, maybe in ten or twenty years' time, it would carry the day in a second referendum. That has been the pattern in the past over devolution. The 1970s devolution referendum was inconclusive but twenty years later, after discontent with Scotland's constitutional arrangements had been ignored, there was a clear majority in favour.

If Scotland is to stay in the UK in the longer term, something must be done to meet the aspirations of those who do not vote for independence but want a greater degree of devolution. Some of what has been suggested, in Devo-Max for example, seems to me to be incompatible with remaining within the UK. But there are things that could be done to strengthen devolution. Entrenching the Scottish Parliament, so that it could not be abolished on a whim of Westminster and making it sovereign in those matters it controls, was the suggestion of the Devo-Plus group and also of the Campbell Committee. As suggested above, more taxation powers than those resulting from the 2012 Act might be devolved and, with them, a part of responsibility for welfare policy. But I suspect that some at least of the discontent that has led to a desire for independence, or more devolution, stems from a general undefined feeling of injustice as a result of the increasing dominance of London both politically and economically in the United Kingdom. Specifically, there has been uneasiness that the dominance of the London financial sector has been accompanied by the decline of industries elsewhere. This feeling is probably even stronger in parts of the north of England and Wales, regions that have done less well economically than Scotland. It points to an urgent need to rebalance the British economy, both geographically and in its structure, so that more emphasis is placed again on manufacturing and less on banking and finance. The policy of trying to promote growth in the regions outside London, on which much emphasis was laid in the 1960s and 1970s, was greatly weakened in the 1980s, when regional development policy was regarded as no longer fitting with the then government's free market philosophy. At the same time, deregulation, including the so-called 'Big Bang', removed most of the previous restrictions on the financial sector. The financial sector has contributed much to the economy in both employment and tax revenue but, in 2008, it nearly brought the country to ruin and we are still suffering from the effects. It is time to alter the balance for the sake of all parts of the United Kingdom.

Notes

Chapter 1 – How Well Off Are We?

1. Scottish Executive, *Scottish Abstract of Statistics*, No 5 (Edinburgh, 1975).
2. The Scottish Office, *Scottish Economic Bulletin* (various years).
3. *Scottish Abstract of Statistics* (various years). For estimates of GDP per head in 1960 and throughout the 1950s, see my *Scotland's Economic Progress 1951–1960* (London, George Allen and Unwin, 1965), pp. 32–6.
4. As reported on 20 March 2013.
5. OECD statistics of GDP per head in purchasing power parity. Data may also be obtained from IMF and the World Bank, which include more countries.
6. Scottish Government, *Government Expenditure and Revenue Scotland 2011–12* (March 2013).
7. Alex Kemp, *The Official History of North Sea Oil and Gas* (Abingdon, Routledge, 2012).
8. Commission on Devolution in Wales (Silk Commission), *Empowerment and Responsibility: Financial Powers to Strengthen Wales* (Cardiff, November 2012); NI Department of Finance & Personnel, *Northern Ireland Net Fiscal Balance Report 2009–10 and 2010–11* (Bangor, County Down, November 2012).
9. Scottish Government, op. cit., p. 45.
10. I analysed this subject in detail in 'Scotland's Public Finances from Goschen to Barnett', *Fraser of Allander Institute Quarterly Economic Commentary*, Vol. 24, No. 2 (March 1999).
11. *Central Scotland: A programme for Development and Growth*, Cmnd 2188 (London, HMSO, November 1963) and *The North-East: A Programme for Development and Growth*, Cmnd 2206 (London, HMSO, November 1963).

12. Scottish Government, *Government Expenditure and Revenue Scotland 2011–2012* (Edinburgh, March 2013).
13. Scottish Government, op. cit., p. 40.
14. Commission on Scottish Devolution (Calman Commission), *Serving Scotland Better: Scotland and the United Kingdom in the 21st Century* (June 2009). Independent Commission on Funding and Finance for Wales (Holtham Commission), *Fairness and Accountability: A New Funding Settlement for Wales* (Cardiff, 2010).
15. Oral evidence taken before the committee on 17 April 2012.
16. Scottish Government, *A National Conversation – Your Scotland, Your Voice* (November 2009), p. 38 ff.

Chapter 2 – Devo-Max, Devo-Plus and the Status Quo

1. HM Government, *Strengthening Scotland's Future*, Cm 7973, TSO (2012).
2. Commission on Scottish Devolution, Final Report, *Serving Scotland Better: Scotland and the United Kingdom in the 21st Century* (June 2009).
3. *Strengthening Scotland's Future*, op. cit., p. 23.
4. Ibid., p. 25.
5. Ibid., p. 23.
6. *Strengthening Scotland's Future*, op. cit., pp. 36–40.
7. Report of a committee under the chairmanship of Sir Menzies Campbell, 'Federalism: the Best Future for Scotland' (Scottish Liberal Democrats, 2009).
8. *Your Scotland, Your Voice*, op. cit.
9. Available on the website of the David Hume Institute.
10. Ibid.
11. Andrew Hughes Hallett and Drew Scott, *Scotland a New Fiscal Settlement*, GMU School of Public Policy Research Paper No. 2010–15 (3 June 2010).
12. Reform Scotland, *A New Union* (Edinburgh, Third Report of the Devo-Plus Group, 2012).
13. Scottish Liberal Democrats, op. cit.
14. Alan Trench, *Devo-More: Fiscal Options for Strengthening the Union* (IPPR, January 2013).
15. Scottish Government, *Fiscal Autonomy in Scotland* (Edinburgh, 2009).

16. Independent Commission on Funding and Finance for Wales, Fairness and Accountability: A New Funding Settlement for Wales (July 2010).

Chapter 3 – The Scope for an Independent Economic Policy

1. Scottish Government, *Corporation Tax: Discussion Paper. Options for Reform* (August 2011).
2. *Government Expenditure and Revenue Scotland 2011–2012*, Scottish Government (Edinburgh, March 2013).
3. Scottish Government, Fiscal Commission Working Group, *First Report – Macroeconomic Framework* (Edinburgh, 2013).
4. *The Irish Times* (9 August 1938).
5. Conor McCabe, *Sins of the Father: Tracing the Decisions that Shaped the Irish Economy* (Dublin, The History of Ireland Press, 2011).
6. Fiscal Commission, op. cit.
7. Reported in *The Scotsman* on 21 February 2013.
8. Ray Perman, *Hubris: How HBOS Wrecked the Best Bank in Britain* (Edinburgh, Birlinn Ltd, 2012).
9. IMF, *World Economic Outlook* (October 2010).
10. IMF, *Fiscal Monitor Update* (July 2012).
11. Dawn Holland and Jonathan Portes, 'Self-defeating Austerity', *National Institute Economic Review*, No. 222 (October 2012).

Chapter 4 – Scotland and Europe

1. John Kerr (Lord Kerr of Kinlochard), 'Don't Count on It: Scotland if independent could not assume that rejoining the EU would be easy – or cheap', *Prospect Magazine* (23 January 2013). See also a fuller version on the Scottish Constitutional Forum Blog (30 January 2013).
2. Sir David Edward's view is posted on the Scottish Constitutional Forum Blog (17 December 2012).
3. HM Government, *Scotland Analysis: Devolution and the Implications of Scottish Independence*, Cm 8554, (February 2013).
4. European Commission, *EU Budget 2011: Financial Report* (Brussels, 2012).
5. HM Treasury, *European Union Finances 2012*, Cm 8405 (July 2012).

6. European Commission, op. cit.

7. Committee of Inquiry into *The Future of Scotland's Hills and Islands* (Royal Society of Edinburgh, September 2008).

8. See the report of the Royal Society of Edinburgh Inquiry which I chaired, *The Future for Scotland's Hills and Islands* (Edinburgh, 2008).

9. The problems of fisheries policy were thoroughly analysed in the report of the Royal Society of Edinburgh's *Inquiry into the Future of the Scottish Fishing Industry* (March 2004).

10. Many of these issues were discussed in the Royal Society of Edinburgh's *Inquiry into the Future of the Scottish Fishing Industry*, of which I was vice chairman (March 2004).

11. See, for instance, Jean-Claude Piris's excellent book, *The Future of Europe* (Cambridge, Cambridge University Press, 2012).

Chapter 5 – Could an Independent Scotland Have Handled the Failure of the Banks?

1. Ray Perman, *Hubris: How HBOS Wrecked the Best Bank in Britain*, op. cit.

2. Robert Peston and Laurence Knight, *How Do We Fix This Mess?* (London, Hodder & Stoughton, 2012).

3. His readiness to lend is well set out in Robert Peston's *Who Runs Britain?* (London, Hodder and Stoughton, 2008).

4. Roger Boyes, *Meltdown Iceland* (London, Bloomsbury, 2009).

5. David J. Lynch, *When the Luck of the Irish Ran Out* (New York, Palgrave Macmillan, 2010) and Conor McCabe, *Sins of the Father*, especially Chapter 5.

6. Final Report of the Independent Commission on Banking, Chairman Sir John Vickers, 12 September 2011.

7. Peston and Knight, *How Do We Fix This Mess?*

8. The details and comparisons are fully set out in my book with Mark Stephens, *Housing Policy in Britain and Europe* (London, UCL Press, 1995).

Chapter 6 – Scotland's Energy Future

1. Scottish Environmental Protection Agency, *State of Scotland's Environment 2006* (Stirling, October 2006).

2. www.sepa.org.uk, *A Climate Change Plan*.

3. Lord Nicholas Stern, *The Economics of Climate Change: The Stern Review* (Cambridge, Cambridge University Press, 2007).
4. Scottish Government, *Energy in Scotland: A Compendium of Energy Statistics* (May, 2012).
5. Royal Society of Edinburgh, *Inquiry into Energy Issues for Scotland* (June 2006).
6. Department of Energy and Climate Change, *Energy Trends* (December 2012).
7. House of Commons Select Committee on Energy and Climate Change, oral evidence from Dr David Kennedy, Chief Executive Committee on Climate Change (19 November 2012).
8. Scottish Hydropower Resource Study (2008).
9. Reported in *The Scotsman*, 10 January 2013.
10. International Energy Agency, *World Energy Outlook 2012*.
11. House of Commons Select Committee on Energy and Climate Change, Mr Francis Egan of Cuadrilla Resources in oral evidence (11 December 2012).

Chapter 7 – North Sea Oil – the Mishandling of an Opportunity

1. Scottish Government, *Government Expenditure and Revenue Scotland 2011–2012* (Edinburgh, March 2013).
2. This is based on the median line in the North Sea between England and Scotland used in estimates made by Alex Kemp and Linda Stephen of Aberdeen University. Scotland's share depends not only on how the line is drawn but on the price of oil and the output of particular fields in any one year. See Alex Kemp's memorandum submitted to the House of Commons Select Committee on Energy and Climate Change, Session 2011–2013.
3. For example, *The Observer* on two successive Sundays in February 1974 in the run-up to the election.
4. Alex Kemp, *The Official History of North Sea Oil and Gas*.
5. Ibid. and House of Commons Select Committee on Energy and Climate Change, oral evidence taken on 17 April, 2012.
6. Based on OECD figures for GDP (see Chapter 1).
7. Unlike my earlier 1974 paper, this one has not been made public.
8. Alex Kemp, *The Official History of North Sea Oil and Gas*.
9. Ibid., Vol. 1, pp. 584–95.
10. As reported in *The Scotsman*, 28 February 2013.
11. *The Scotsman* (16 January 2013).

Chapter 8 – Welfare and Inequality

1. John Curtice and Rachel Ormiston, *Attitudes towards Scotland's Constitutional Future*, Scottish Social Attitudes Survey (ScotCen, January 2013).
2. Professor Bell's paper is available on the David Hume Institute website.
3. Department for Work and Pensions, *Universal Credit: Impact Assessment (1A)* (December 2012).
4. Jim McCormick's report, 'Welfare "Reform" and Mitigation in Scotland', for the Scottish Council of Voluntary Organisations, (January 2013).
5. David Bell, op. cit.
6. Hannah Aldridge, Peter Kenway and Tom MacInnes, 'Monitoring Poverty and Social Exclusion Scotland 2013' (Joseph Rowntree Foundation, 2013).
7. Jonathan Cribb, Robert Joyce and David Phillips, 'Living Standards, Poverty and Inequality in the UK' (Joseph Rowntree Foundation for the Institute for Fiscal Studies, 2012).
8. Ibid.
9. Lesley Riddoch writing in *The Scotsman* has argued for the Scandinavian model and Joyce McMillan for a more equal society.
10. See, for example, Alan Trench, 'Funding Devo-More: Fiscal Options for Strengthening the Union' (IPPR, January 2013).

Chapter 9 – Conclusion

1. Reported in *The Scotsman*, 7 March 2013.
2. See John Kay's article in *The Scotsman*, (7 March 2013) and his excellent chapter in *Scotland's Future: the Economics of Constitutional Change* (Dundee, Dundee University Press, 2013).
3. Commission on Scottish Devolution, *Serving Scotland Better* (Edinburgh, 2009), p. 97.

Index